SEVILLE

SEVILLE

Series editor
Michael Shichor

I *NBAL*
Travel Information Ltd.

Inbal Travel Information Ltd.
P.O.Box 39090 Tel Aviv Israel 61390

Intl. ISBN 965-288-081-7

Distributed in the United Kingdom by:
Kuperard (London) Ltd.
9, Hampstead West
224 Iverson Road
West Hampstead
London NW6 2HL

U.K. ISBN 1-85733-021-8

CONTENTS

*T*ABLE OF MAPS

Preface

During the Middle Ages the Iberian peninsula was the arena of a long drawn struggle between West and East, between Christianity and Islam. This struggle was particularly long and bitter in Andalusia, where the first Moslim tribes landed from North Africa in the 8th century — and where they lost their last battle against the Catholic Kings, in 1492.

That year is also the date of Christopher Columbus' first voyage of discovery toward the Western Indies, an event that marks, for the whole world, the beginning of a new era, the birth of the "New World" — and brought to Seville, the Capital of Andalusia, an epoch of great glory.

Five centuries later, in 1992, Seville has been called to host the greatest ever world exhibition — EXPO 92. An event that has brought to Seville an unprecedented building boom, due to revolutionize all aspects of that city's economic infrastructure and daily life.

This guide attempts to highlight Seville's many enchanting faces, its hidden jewels and its life and history, from its Roman days to the present. During your visit you'll doubtlessly come to sense the paradox of this great country — the new Spain, getting ready in earnest for the coming of the twenty-first century, while jealously preserving the traditions and glories of past centuries.

The preparation of this comprehensive and detailed volume has engaged many experts, and thanks to them we are proud to present you with a work as precise and updated as possible, in days of such unparalleled growth as Seville is living even now. We are deeply grateful to them all, and especially to Eliezer Novodvorski, who contributed to this volume his wide knowledge and expertise in all fields of local life, history and culture.

Our work will not only acquaint you with the world famous wines of Jerez, the best menus of Andalusian kitchen, and the famous sights of Old Seville; but will also help you explore and experience the dinamic pulse of Seville and Spain, in this last decade of our century, so rich of promise for the next.

Michael Shichor

Using this Guide

In order to reap maximum benefit from the information concentrated in this Guide, we advise the traveller to carefully read the following advice and to act upon it. The facts contained in this book are meant to help the tourist find his way around, and to assure that he sees the most, with maximum savings of money, time and effort.

The information contained in the Introduction should be read in its entirety as it will supply you with details which will help in making early decisions and arrangements for your trip. Reviewing the material thoroughly, and acting upon it, means that you will be more organized and set for your visit. Upon arrival, you will already feel familiar and comfortable with Seville.

The basic guideline in all MICHAEL'S GUIDE publications is to survey places in a primarily geographical sequence. The detailed introductory chapters discuss general topics and specific aspects of getting organised. The tour routes, laid out geographically, lead the visitor along the city's streets, providing a survey of the sights and sounds of the twentieth century and step deepen one's familiarity with Seville, and make a visit there so much more enjoyable. A concise list of "Musts" follows, describing those sites without which a visit to Seville is not complete.

We have also included a selection of excursions, which are all interesting and worth a visit. Each of these excursions makes for a very pleasant day trip out of Seville.

The numerous maps which accompany the tour routes have been especially prepared, and show the visitor exactly how to reach the sites and attractions discussed in the tour routes.

Since Seville is a highly esteemed for its gourmet cuisine, Spanish wines, fine shopping and entertainment, we have devoted a special chapter to "Making the most of your stay" in the city. Here you will find a broad range of possibilities, to suit your budget, which will help you enjoy your stay.

To further facilitate the use of this Guide, we have included a detailed index at the back of the book, which lists all the major sites, and refers you to the place where each site is discussed in greatest detail.

Because times change, and cities are dynamic, an important rule when travelling, especially to a vibrant city like Seville, should be to consult local sources of information. Although we have made every effort to confirm that facts are up-to-date, changes do occur and travellers may find certain facts somewhat inaccurate when arriving at their destinations, and for this we apologize in advance.

In order to be as up to date as possible, cooperation and assistance are necessary from those of you who have enjoyed the information contained in this Guide. For this purpose we have included a short questionnaire at the end of the Guide, and will be most grateful to those who complete it and send it to us.

During your visit you will see and experience many things — we have therefore left several blank pages at the back of the Guide. These are for you, to jot down those special experiences of people and places, feelings and significant happenings along the way.

Have a pleasant and exciting trip!

*I*NTRODUCTION

Part One — Getting to Know Seville

History

The fertile valley of the Guadalquivir river, with its wide open spaces and rolling hills, has always attracted shepherds, hunters, farmers, fishermen and sailors from all over the Iberian Peninsula as well as from other nations.

Seville has a history as colourful as its scenery: its blue rivercourse, its rich gold-yellow Andalusian soil, its sunshine, its verdant gardens, its bullfights and its treasures: Roman roads and ruins, Moorish arabesques and wells, Renaissance palaces, Columbian gold, Jewish, Muslem and Catholic shrines.

First findings

Some of the archaeological excavations carried out in Seville and the vicinity have uncovered signs of human settlement as early as the beginning of the Neolithic Period. Apparently, the first permanent dwellings were set along the great blue river more than 4000 years ago. During the Bronze Age — 2500 years ago — the rich mineral layers of the Guadalquivir hills attracted local greedy miners and adventurous seafarers from the eastern Mediterranean — the Phoenicians. In fact Seville's name was coined from the ancient semitic word for "plain" (*shephela* in Hebrew, *saphilla* in Aramaic).

The Phoenician sailors were overwhelmed by the beauty and wealth of the region. On their return, they praised it so volubly that soon many other adventurers and traders sailed from Greece to the prosperous new land. The traders settled in, and left their imprint on the Andalusian soil and on the local culture and lore.

The most remarkable archaeological finds relate to the

INTRODUCTION

Tartessian culture (seventh century BC), and are on the Carambolo Hill, very close to modern Seville. The Tartessians were a rural tribe that also dabbled in mining and sheep-herding. Ambitious Greek traders must have bartered and haggled with the Tartessians for more than three centuries; not much remains, however, of that epoch, except for some outstandingly sophisticated gold ornaments and jewels. A remarkable collection of the Treasure of Carambolo is displayed at the Seville Archaeological Museum (see "From the Centre to the Maria Luisa Park").

The Tartessian culture disappeared with the arrival of a new wave of immigrants: after the First Punic War, the people of Carthago, fleeing from the victorious Roman legions, crossed the straits from Africa in search of a new home. The newcomers settled in the Guadalquivir valley, where they began preparing for the second round of the Rome-Carthago struggle.

In 218 BC, Hannibal, at the head of the most powerful army of his times, crossed the Iberic Peninsula, the Pyrenees Mountains and the Alps and invaded Italy. The outcome of his brilliant campaign, however, ended in failure: after winning the first skirmishes along the way, his tired and deplated army was utterly defeated in what would come to be known as the Russian Napoleonic syndrome by the Romans. Meanwhile, Rome had sent a relatively small expedition to Southern Iberia, easily overcoming the scanty defences Hannibal had left behind to protect the local settlements. Scipio, the Roman leader, was thus able to establish the Roman Iberic Province of Hispania in 206, which extended over the entire southern half of the peninsula.

As did their predecessors, the Romans fell in love with the Guadalquivir Valley, and founded the town of Italica, which is 5 miles north of present day Seville. It soon became the capital of the Roman Province of Hispania.

Seville owes its first urbanisation to Julius Ceasar. In 45 BC, he laid the founding stone of the new Roman town of Julia Romulea, on the ruins of the ancient Greek-Phoenician acropolis. The statue of Ceasar is present in Seville, standing in the Alameda de Hércules, next to statue of Heracles — the mythological founder of the city.

The Roman geographer Strabon (64 BC-25 AD), describes the region as follows: "...even the largest trading ships can enter the Hispalis by the river, bringing supplies and loading products at all the upriver towns. All along the river the land is green and fertile, and incomparably well cultivated. The hills outlining the valley are covered with all sorts of trees and other natural shrubs."

The Hispanic Province continued to prosper until the fall of the Roman Empire. Then, in the 5th century AD, the Vandals raided the peninsula, crossing the straits from Africa. Later, in the 6th century, the Visigoths arrived from across the Pyreneen Mountains and swept the whole Iberian Peninsula. Neither of them touched Seville; on the contrary, it became the Visigoth Capital of the Betica Province (present day Andalusia), while their central government settled in Toledo. In 589 the Visigoth King Recaredo adopted Christianity and Seville became the home of the great Archbishopric of San Isidoro and San Leandro. Visigoth Seville prospered and grew. After less than two centuries, however, the Visigoth Kingdom lost its power.

The Moslem Period

The force of the new Islamic faith practically swept through the entire Middle East. Towards the end of the 7th century, it changed course to the western reaches of the Mediterranean and North Africa.

Legitimization of the Islamic conquest was provided in 710 by the Visigoth King of Iberia. He was threatened by mass insurrection, and turned to the Moors for help. The crossing by the Islamic Army led by Tark-ibn Ziyad gave the strait its modern name of Gibraltar (*Jebbel-el-Tark* — The Mount of Tark).

The Moorish Tribes (the name given to the invading Moslem tribes crossing over from Africa into Iberia) gradually occupied and settled in most of the peninsula (except the northern province of Asturia), and even crossed the Pyrenees and settled along the French coast. Betica, one of the first regions conquered by the Moors, was called "El-Andalus" ("the Vandals'"), and

*I*NTRODUCTION

then, simply, became "Andalucía". The first tribes that settled in the region were of Yemenite origine. For the first half of the 8th century Andalusia was ruled by the eastern Caliphate of Baghdad. In 756 one of the local chieftains, Abed-el-Rahman, was able to claim the independence from Baghdad of the Iberian provinces, and set himself up in Cordoba as Caliph Abed-el-Rahman of the Western Islamic Empire.

Cordoba was too far away from Baghdad, and the Oriental potentates obviously preferred to acquiesce peacefully to the claims of western independence. Thus the unique example of a religion-based kingdom was born, in which the believers of all other monotheistic faiths were free to practice their religions and beliefs, and to grow and prosper together to unprecedented levels of cultural and economic affluence.

Engineering, architecture, literature, poetry, philosophy, mathematics, linguistics, as well as other realms of human knowledge flourished and outgrew the standards of their European counterparts.

Seville, whose name was then Ixbilia, was one of the major provincial centres of the Cordoba Caliphate. The river became the Guadalquivir ("Wadi-el Kebir" — the Great Stream).

In 844 a Norman fleet entered the Guadalquivir, sacking Seville and butchering thousands of people. But soon the city recovered, building new walls and ramparts, on which the great Alcázar was later erected.

During the 10th century, Seville was one of the most prosperous towns in the richest kingdom of Europe. But in the next century the central administration of Cordoba faltered, and the Caliphate was dismembered into a number of *taifas* (regional or local feuds). Seville established itself as an independent kingdom under the Abbadi dynasty; in 1069, under King Al Mutamid, Seville became the most important and richest *taifa* in the entire peninsula; the Great Alcázar built by Al Mutamid, served as his royal residence.

Less than twenty years after Al Mutamid's coronation, in 1085, Toledo fell to the invading Christian armies advancing from the north. The Seville Moors invited the Almoravids, North-African Moslems, to cross the straits and assist them in the eventual defense of the province. The invitation was more than welcome: only six years later the Almoravides ousted the former rulers and took the city into their own hands. Their rule lasted for less than half a century: another North African Moslem tribe, the Almohades, having heard of the wonders of Seville, also crossed the straits and took over the city. The Almohades were great builders, and Seville owes them a large Mosque (later transformed into Seville's Cathedral) and its outstanding minaret (see "The Cathedral").

The Moors ruled Seville for more than five centuries (712-1248). Their contributions to literature, architecture, administration, and agriculture made Seville one of the most advanced and admired cities of its times.

The Christian Conquest
When the Christians were ousted from almost the entire Iberian peninsula territory, they were able to hold a narrow strip of soil, far in the north, the Asturias. From their northern stronghold, having licked their wounds for more than five centuries, the Asturians got ready for the "Reconquista" of Spain. It was a long-drawn out battle, which ended with the total expulsion of the Moors in 1492, when the last stronghold of Granada fell to the Christian Kings.

The Moslem rulers, too deeply involved with cultural and administrative progress in their own territory, had neglected to keep an alert eye on the north. The little Asturian kingdom in the far north had thus been given the opportunity to expand slowly southward. With every new conquest, the Christians built a network of new castles — which ended by giving the kingdom its new name: Castilla.

The Christian *Reconquista* had already made its first step in the 11th century, when the call to arms launched by the Pope against the Moslem infidels roused Ferdinand I of Castilla to a local Crusade against the Moors. Thirty years later, in 1085, Alfonso VI conquered Toledo, which became his new Capital.

In 1212, the Moors finally reacted, forming a united army

in Seville, which challenged the Christians at Las Navas de Tolosa. The battle ended with the complete rout of the Moors, leaving the whole of Andalusia at the mercy of the Christian forces. Cordoba fell to the Christians in 1236, and ten years later Seville found itself under siege. The city resisted for almost 15 months, but in November 1248 the city's defences failed to stem a breach led by one of King Ferdinand III's chieftains, Bonifaz, along the Guadalquivir. The two main river forts fell, and the representatives of the city surrendered, presenting the Christian King with the keys of the city (still on show at the Cathedral).

The Christian Rule

The return of Christiendom brought to Seville a new socio-political climate — as it did to the rest of the Peninsula. Mosques, minarets and other palaces were soon transformed into churches, belltowers and monasteries. The Mezquita Mayor (Great Mosque) became a church. King Alfonso X, "El Sabio" ("The Wise"), added new gothic wings to the Alcazar. Seville became the chosen seat of many a Spanish King. Don Pedro "El Cruel", who was probably the father of Spanish Absolutism, established his own royal residence in a new wing inside the Alcázar; he also built the great Convento de Santa Clara (Monastery of Santa Clara) and several other palaces.

During the 14th century Seville was one of Spain's main administrative centres, and the building boom took on new dimensions. King Ferdinand V of Aragon and Isabella I of Castilla regarded Seville as a sort of "winter capital". Their marriage, which united their kingdoms, made Spain one of the major powers in Europe.

Their period is known as the Era of the Catholic Kings — and of the Inquisition. Infidels and heretics were tortured and executed in scores of city squares throughout the kingdom. The Jews, who for centuries had contributed to the culture and administration of the country, were expelled from Spain in 1492 — the same year that Christopher Columbus set out, with royal blessings, toward the West Indies, to discover the land that would be named America.

*I*NTRODUCTION

Upon Columbus' return, Seville became the exclusive centre of Spanish trade with its newly discovered overseas colonies. Later westward voyages, by Columbus, Amerigo Vespucci and Magellan, were planned and launched from Seville, which had become the unchallenged capital of the Colonies. In that period Seville reached the peak of its prosperity, and the new great city hall was built in 1527.

This was Spain's golden age, with Carlos I (who, under the name of Roman Christian Emperor Charles V ruled the whole of Western Europe) and with Philip II. During their time, Spain was Europe's greatest power, and its navy reached the shores of four continents. In 1561 Madrid became the capital of Spain, and Seville found itself gradually sinking back to the dimensions of a provincial town. While it remained the main centre of trade with the colonies, soon the impact of the growing acts of piracy at sea, encouraged and often sponsored by the English Crown, had a catastrophic effect on the welfare of the city.

After the rout of the Spanish Navy — the Great Armada (1588) — Spain lost much of its political and military power, and Seville recovered some of its fame as a centre of arts, culture and study in the 17th century. Some of the greatest names of that epoch worked and lived in Seville: the best known are the painters Murillo and Velazquez — and Cervantes, creator of the universally celebrated *Don Quixote de la Mancha.*

When Carlos II died in 1700, he was succeeded by the Bourbon dynasty (an offshoot of the Habsburgs). In 1717 Seville was deprived of its traditional monopoly of colonial trade, and the colonial office was transferred to Cadiz. In 1755, an earthquake devastated the city, and four years later the Guadalquivir flooded what was left, causing further damage. In 1800, a jaundice epidemic killed one third of Seville's population.

In 1808, King Carlos IV abdicated in favour of his son Ferdinand VII. Only a few years later he appealed to Napoleon, hoping to recover the throne with his assistance. The French emperor summoned father and son to Bayonne, and forced them both to step down in favour of his brother, Joseph Bonaparte, who, at the head of a French army, was already on the way to Madrid. On 2 May the people of Madrid rose in arms against their French conquerors. The rebellion was bitterly quelled, but its seeds were sown throughout the country. A wave of armed resistance to the French swept the country, forcing Joseph Bonaparte to flee for his life only two months later. Napoleon himself undertook a punitive campaign, reconquering the land and reinstating his brother as king of Madrid. The surviving nucleus of Spanish resistance fled to Seville, where it was forced to surrender to Soult's French army. The French occupied Seville for two years, until 1812, when the Napoleonic Empire was already doomed.

The End of Absolutism
The French had been expelled from Spain, but the spirit of the French Revolution thrived, bringing in a new aura of liberalism. When Ferdinand VII returned to his throne in 1814, he was enthusiastically welcomed by the people — but as soon as he attempted to ban the new statutes, trying to re-establish the past glories of the monarchy, the mood of the people changed.

Ferdinand died in 1833, and a war of succession broke out between his liberal daughter Isabella II — and the dead king's royalist brother Don Carlos. The armed struggle continued for several years, playing havoc throughout Spain. The Church's properties were confiscated; one of the major monasteries of Seville was transformed into an industrial complex (see "Expo '92"). The unrest continued for several decades, with the weakened central power changing hands several times.

In 1868, Isabella was finally overthrown by a military coup, and in 1873 a republican administration was appointed by the junta. The new government survived for less than two years, and in 1875 Isabella's son Alfonso was crowned, under the name of King Alfonso XII.

At Alfonso's death, in 1885, his widow was pregnant with his son and Crown Prince. Maria Cristina of Austria ruled in his place until 1902, when the youth was finally crowned as King Alfonso XIII.

The Spanish colonial empire in the Americas and in Asia had come to an end in 1898. It happened at a time when even the weaker colonies had been granted independence by the Spanish government, since it was unable to cope with its administrative functions. This development damaged Seville's status and affluence. Even Seville's attempt to host the Ibero-American Fair, at the new Maria Luisa Park (see "From the Centre of town to the Maria Luisa Park") in 1929 did not reinstate Seville as the Capital of Ibero-American Trade.

The already weakened constitutional monarchy fell in 1930, and in 1931 the Republic of Spain was established, in an atmosphere of growing social unrest. Unemployment was rampant, especially in the south and in the larger urban centres. A long delayed rural reform got under way. In Seville an open rebellion broke out in the popular quarter of Triana. The city became the main stronghold of the Anarchist Party. But the Church rallied its forces, siding with the feudal aristocracy, against the anarchists and other leftist groups.

In 1936, it became clear that the republican administration had totally lost the reins of government. Murders and acts of terror were the order of the day. The army was divided. The Church, the aristocracy and the royalists found themselves on a united front against anarchists, republicans and communists. On 18 July 1936, in Seville, general Queipo de Llanos intervened to quell insurrection in Triana, and took over the administration of the city.

Triana was completely destroyed, and in spite of the people's widespread allegiance to the Republic, the city fell to the alliance of Church and royalists. During the following three years, while civil war raged throughout Spain, Seville remained in the hands of Generalissimo Franco's right-wing party, and therefore saved itself from the scourge of war.

Modern Seville
With the active help of the "new order" states — Hitler's Germany and Mussolini's Italy — Franco's iron

rule smothered all opposition. For many years Franco concentrated his efforts on the survival of his own regime. The country's progress came to a halt, and gradually became one of the most backward countries in the West. Standards of living were among the lowest in Europe; agriculture and industry struggled to maintain levels more suitable to the 19th than to the mid-20th century. Seville survived as a backwater centre of Spanish aristocracy, but the brunt of world depression, unemployment and poverty was clearly evident.

In the 60s, world tourism re-discovered Seville, kindling a new wave of hotel-construction and growth, that in the 70s swept the whole of Spain. Franco's regime died with him, on 17th November, 1975.

Spain rejoined the family of European nations. After the election of a democratic government, the country reached the industrial and economic standards of the European Community in the span of a few years. A native Sevillan, Philip Gonzales, head the Spanish Socialist Party, easily won all his country's general elections of 1982.

Seville — facts and figures
Seville lies on the banks of the Guadalquivir River. The sources of that river stem from the Sierra de Cazorla Mountains, whose peaks reach about 5,000 feet. The Alfonso XIII Canal cuts the town in two, creating the island of La Cartuja between the river and the canal. It also provides Seville with a navigable outlet to the Atlantic Ocean, 60 miles south-west of the city.

Seville is surrounded by a wide and exceptionally fertile plain, with hundreds of villages and dense rural centres over an area of more than 6,000 square miles. With a population of 650,000, Seville is the fourth largest city in Spain. The rural population of the province accounts for more than 1,000,000 people — or about 20% of the population of Andalusia.

Spain is subdivided into several partially autonomous regions; Seville is the capital of Andalusia, and as such is the seat of the Andalusian Parliament and regional administration. The Sevillians cast their votes in three separate polls: for their Mayor, for the Andalusian Parliament and at the General Elections of Spain. The King and Queen are highly honoured guests of the city, and they keep a Royal Apartment at the Alcázar Palace.

The climate

Seville has the hottest climate in Spain. In July and August maximum temperatures often reach the nineties (F), with occasional peaks of up to 110F. The city and its people do their best to adapt to their torrid climate, and after lunch everybody retires to a well earned (and protracted) *siesta*.

Winter is very temperate, with pleasant temperatures around the sixties (F). The annual precipitations average 20 inches, all of them during the winter.

The economy

As previously mentioned, the fertile Guadalquivir plain has attracted wandering tribes and farming cultures from all parts of the peninsula and past its borders for centuries. Agriculture has always been — and still is — one of Seville's main interests, even in its hey-day as the exclusive centre of Spanish colonial trade.

The Sevillan province is farmed intensively, with 20% of its population directly involved in farming. Among the main local produce there is grain, cotton, citrus fruits and olives. Until recently most of the land belonged to a few baronial families, who used to parcel it off for farming to hundreds of tenants. Lately part of the land has been apportioned to rural coops — but even today thousands of people are employed in farming as daily labourers, at incredibly low wages.

Rural unemployment is among the highest in Spain. Andalusia is one of the major backwater regions of modern Spain. One of the main efforts of the Spanish administration is to lead Seville into the mainstream of modern western civilization. The decision to hold the great Expo '92 Fair in Seville is part of this effort.

Seville's second main income comes from tourism. More than one million foreign tourists visit Seville every year — in addition to hundreds of thousands of Spaniards.

INTRODUCTION

Hotel construction is several years behind the hectic growth of local tourism, and Seville hotels are chronically overcrowded and proverbially antiquated. Thanks to the Expo '92 project, billions of $US have found their way to land and building development, and there are hopes that the fair will help contribute to a new era of Sevillan tourism. Other international events will follow, and the number of visitors from abroad will at least double in the next few seasons.

Industry comes third — after farming and tourism. Not many industrial initiatives have been able to prosper. Even those that did, are labour-based industries, employing untrained and unqualified manpower, mainly in textile and food commodities, at very low wages. Andalusia, and the Sevillan province, are among the major exporters of Spanish olive oil. Only 10% of the labour force is employed in industry, and industrial growth is as of yet very slow.

Culture and arts
Seville is for many a personification of all that is Spanish; summer heat, temperament, corridas and flamenco, sensuality and bigotry, gothic towers and moorish courtyards — symmetry and contrast. These are the things we aim to show you through this guide. And these are the things that have brought so many great men of art and culture to love this city and to spend some of their best years in it, seeking memories and echoes of past glories.

Architecture
Even at first sight, Seville's old streets and palaces, transmit an almost magic synthesis between different epochs, peoples and cultures. Almost three millennia of history have contributed to create present-day Seville.

Very little remains of Roman times, except for the ruins of Italica, 4 miles off the city on the Merida road (see "Excursions"). Here, in this garrison town erected by Scipio's victorious legions, you will see several striking mosaics, a large number of marble capitols and columns and an impressive amphitheatre, a good example of the Roman style characteristic of the 1st century BC. In

*I*NTRODUCTION

Seville itself, the glories of this period have disappeared under the accomplishments of so many later cultures and builders.

Seville owes many of its sites and facets to the Moors. Of the many architects and builders, artists and scientists, mathematicians and theologists, it was the Moors who crossed the straits from North Africa to Spain on the wake of Mohammed's triumph leaving their indelible imprint on Seville. Thanks to them, Seville became the first lady of Spain, a centre of spiritual life, of study and of trade — and became one of the most civilized and richest kingdoms of its times. This is clearly reflectd in the buildings left behind. The Moors built with an eye for striking contrast of stark sunlight and dark shadows. In the heart of their sunny palaces you will see the cool spaces of well-sheltered patios and courtyards, where the dark green vegetation contrasts with the yellowish glare of the sunswept plains. Often impressive fountains underscore the contrast, hinting at man's leisurely victory over nature. The windows are small, as if to admit an essential measure of light, while preventing the onslaught of torrid sunrays. The Islam abhors human images and statues, and its sense of art and beauty is expressed in symbolical, geometrical ornamentation in wood and stone, set upon walls and arches and stucco ceilings. In most cases, even the frequent Arab inscriptions assume an ornamental character.

The most prominent and most representative element of Moorish architecture is the mosque. Only later, when Seville become an independent kingdom, Moorish architecture also found expression in other structures, such as the **Great Alcázar**, the **Torre del Oro** and the **Giralda Minaret**.

After the Christian *Reconquista*, toward the second half of the 13th century, the new rulers decided to preserve the existing palaces. They fitted them to the requirements of their culture and faith: mosques were turned into churches, other palaces into monasteries. Thus some new elements of Gothic style came to complement the beauty of Moorish architecture, creating a unique harmony of contrasts. This is freely expressed in Christian elements attached to Moorish palaces and in Moorish arabesques decorating the Gothic structures of that epoch. The Great Alcázar, and Don Pedro's Palace, are outstanding examples of this synthesis.

Later, in the 15th century, the Gothic style claimed its final prominence, as can be seen when entering the wide spaces of the great cathedral.

Toward the end of the same century, and at the beginning of the 16th, the unique *Plataresque* style made its appearance in Spain. This style represents the symbiotic expression of Moorish elements within a Gothic mainstream of expression. One of the best examples can be seen in Seville's City Hall.

The Baroc style, which swept Europe during the 17th and 18th centuries, also left its imprint on Seville, not only in a series of new structures, but also in several ambitious projects for the restoration of older buildings. The local Baroc, however, absorbed some of the spirit and expressions of the deeply ingrained Moorish influence, and the outcome was the so-called *Churriguèresque* style (named after the Churriguera Madrid family, the main sponsor of the new style in Andalusia). One of the best examples of this style is the **San Telmo Palace**, built by the famous local architect Leonardo Figueroa.

Among the most impressive product of Baroc architecture we find the San Salvador Church (a completely restored former mosque), the Casa de Pilatos (in which one may recognize the imprints of several different styles), and the Plaza de España, the central square of the Maria Luisa Park. Such structures, that may seem rather bombastic, elsewhere, are in complete harmony with Sevillian landscapes.

One of the main elements of local architecture is the coloured tile, used as a decorative element on the front of many buildings. Coloured tiles may have been used ornamentally as far back as in ancient Egypt — and certainly in Persia. The 7th century wave of Islamic conquest brought this decorative medium to Spain, where it assumed its characteristic azure (in Spanish, *azulejo*) shade. Almost all Andalusian buildings are richly decorated with *azulejo* tiles.

*I*NTRODUCTION

Another characteristic of Andalusian buildings is the predominant use of monochromic wall-painting in white, red or ochre. This tradition has been sanctioned by legislation, and today builders are required to adopt just one of these three colours.

The white *cal* (whitewash) is actually an off-white, almost everchanging hue, brilliant under the sun, soothingly opaque in the dark and almost phosphorescent under moonlight. Its light *se apaga, se aviva y se ahoga* ("switches off, and on, and brightens") and has come to symbolize the Sevillans' longing for innocence and leisure. It goes without saying that *cal* always also had some vital practical functions, like protecting homes from the torrid summer sun and providing some night vision before the era of street lighting.

Seville's dominant colour is amber yellow. It seems almost to merge with the somewhat deeper golden tint of its soil. In the past, before the age of asphalt, even Seville's streets wore the same soft golden hues. The effect is particularly catching at the great bull-fights arena of Maestranza, but it is also apparent along all of Seville's streets and alleys.

Sometimes an array of brilliant reds appears, only to underscore by contrast the everpresent amber of the streets, the deep blue of the sky and the *azulejo* of the majestic buildings. A perfect background for painters and colour photographers — and for all lovers of beauty.

The decorative arts

Art expression during the Middle Ages followed the Islamic precepts, which forbid the use of human images; therefore it limited itself to geometric ornamentation, inscriptions, stylized gardens and water-jets. Later, after the Christian *Reconquista*, religious figurative art became the main form of artistic expression. Later Medieval art — paintings and sculptures in the style of the great Spanish School — is well represented in almost all churches of that period. That school is represented in Seville by Francisco Pacheco (1564-1644), an eminent student, painter (teacher, among others, of Diego Velazquez, 1599-1660), by Alonso Cano (1601-1667) and by Francisco Zurbaran (1622-1690).

*I*_NTRODUCTION_

Bartolome Murillo (1617-1682), a native Sevillan, was a pupil of Velazquez at his Madrid school, but returned to paint in his hometown, together with Valdez Leál (1622-1690).

The statues of these artists, together with many of their paintings, are preserved in several Sevillan museums, and mainly at the Museo de Bellas Artes (see "Seville's Muses").

Literature

Seville often attracted poets and writers from all over Spain and from abroad. It is also the birthplace of Spanish Nobel prize (1977) winned author Vicente Aleixandre (1898-1984). Juan Ramon Jimenez (Nobel Prize for Literature, 1958) was born in 1881 at Palos de Moguer, near Seville.

One of Seville's first great scholars was Isidoro (560-636), author of a fundamental etymologic treaty. Another great Sevillan name is Tirso de Molina (1583-1648), a priest who became one of the fathers of Spanish theatre, author of the classic play *El Burlador de Seville* (1630), prototype of the Don Juan legend, confusingly thought to be based upon the life of the great *bon vivant* Don Miguel de Maniara (see "La Caridad Hospital"). In our century, Antonio Machado (1875-1939), one of Spain's most popular poets, is also one of the most revered Sevillans.

Lope de Vega (1562-1636) wrote *Estrella de Seville*, a tragedy based upon the dilemma of loyalty to the King as opposed to the claims of personal friendship. Cervantes wrote a large part of his *Don Quixote de la Mancha* while he was in Seville. Gustavo Adolfo Becquer (1836-1870) one of the greatest Spanish national poets, also lived for several years in Seville.

The French writer and poet Prosper Mérimée was inspired to write the Carmen saga here in Seville. We can hardly end without a mention to the legendary Figaro, hero of Pierre de Beaumarchais' (1732-1799) and of Mozartian and Rossinian fame.

INTRODUCTION

Music and dance

Seville's romantic aura inspired a great number of dramaturges, poets and novelists; not less than 24 operas are based on this southern Spanish capital. Bizet's *Carmen*, Beethoven's *Fidelio*, Mozart's *Don Juan* and *The Marriage of Figaro*, Rossini's *The Barber of Seville* are among the most well known. The myths, images and lore of Seville cast their spell upon many a writer who never set foot on its soil.

Opera lovers will not miss a visit to the local University Palace (formerly the tobacco plant where Carmen was employed) or a stroll on Plaza Alfaro, where Figaro used to serenade his lovely Rosina.

But Seville's incomparable musical attraction is, of course, the **Flamenco**.

The Flamenco is a unique cocktail of Moorish melody and gypsy rhythm, spiced with lovers' tears and nostalgy.

Its melody flows through the endless trills of a lone singer, accompanied by the beat of guitars and *castañetas*, the steps of riding boots and measured hand-clappings.

The experts distinguish between several types of flamenco: with or without the various trimmings of dancing or clapping; with so many verses and refrains. The *Sevillana* style, sung by one dancer, with *castañetas* in her hands, accompanied by a lone guitarist, has gradually become the most popular, and indeed is internationally recognized as "the" flamenco.

Several Sevillan theatre halls, the *tablaos*, are exclusively dedicated to this form of popular art.

During the Easter week (see "The Holy Week"), the *Saetas*, another Flamenco style, are in full swing, and they perform in period garb at the main squares and crossings of the city centre.

Another speciality of Sevillian music is the *Seises* — a choral of ten children's voices, often heard at most religious festivals, in the Great Cathedral and in other churches, dressed in virginal traditional robes.

"*Seise*" means sixteen — not ten. And in fact, the chorus was once composed of sixteen voices; while the number of singers has been reduced to ten, the name "sixteen" remains unchanged. This ancient tradition was almost abolished by the authorities three centuries ago, after a long period of famine. When the populace protested too loudly, a compromise was struck, and the *Seise* was allowed to continue "until the singer's robes remain whole"; but the people, in great secrecy, renewed them from time to time, and thus the tradition was allowed to survive. In 1820, however, the customary castration of the young singers, mandatory to prevent their final change of voice, was strictly outlawed.

Seville's youngsters do not differ substantially from their counterparts from other parts of Spain and Europe. They are very up-to-date with regard to the various folk, rock, swing and other schools of modern music, but they also have the privilege to be among the very few who've had the opportunity to familiarize themselves with the voices of Joaquin Sabina, Martirio or Paco de Lucia.

The Corridas
The traditional struggle between man (represented by the *torero* or *matador*) and beast (represented by a preferably wild bull) still excites a great majority of the Spanish people and is also one of the major tourist attractions of Spain, and of Seville in particular. The *Corrida* has become a very respected tradition today, following rigid ceremonial rules under the pain of clamorous public outcry.

The tradition is very ancient indeed. It was probably practiced — as *Tauromaquia* — in several ancient civilizations. In its present form, the *Corrida* has remained strictly unchanged for more than two centuries. The arena of the *Maestranza*, in Seville, is one of the oldest and most respected in Spain. No great *torero* will miss the opportunity of a performance at the *Maestranza*.

Not all Spaniards favour this "sport". There is a growing bitter dispute between the traditional groups who wish this custom to be kept alive at all costs — and various humane and other associations, who would bluntly like to end "such a bloody waste of bulls and men".

In fact only the most devoted fans of the *Corrida* appreciate in full the many details of the ceremonial fight, whose final result (the gory death of the bull) is inevitable from the start.

Nevertheless, each *torero* follows his own ritual superstitions, taking the utmost care to wear his traditional uniform (*Traje de luces*) in a fixed, ceremonial manner, accepting (or rejecting) from his fans token offers of herbs and flowers, and addressing himself in prayer to his own god.

After the prayers the *corrida* gets under way. The *torero's* assistants (*picadores* and *banderieros*), make their colourful appearance, and finally the bull (*toro*) himself enters the arena.

Olé cries the incensed audience, and the *matador* begins his ritual steps, pointing his red *capa* (mantle) at the bull, to entice him to an amock charge, that he will avoid, hopefully, by a hair's breadth. This is where the wildly aroused audience will judge whether the *torero* does indeed have what it takes, until the wounded and harassed bull is finally put out of his misery.

Even the final act of the *torero's* sword has its ceremonial aspects: the bull must be put to death with a single, "clean" thrust. Then the victorious *torero* will raise his hat, and throw it to one of the most beautiful girls in the arena, whom he will also present with the longed gift of the bull's left ear...

Then the carcass of the bull is carried off the arena by a team of horses, while the *matador* is covered with flowers and cheered by his admirers. Things are somewhat different, however, if the *torero* himself has to be carried off the arena by medics...

Seville is one of the main centres of this "sport". Scores of restaurants and pubs lining the arena on all sides, cater to the *aficionados* (fans) who crowd them before and after major events. That is where one may listen (in Spanish, of course) to legendary lore and to heroic feats of the most revered *toreros*, and admire the wall posters and pictures of great *corridas* that cover the walls of the premises.

The *corridas* season opens, as we have already mentioned, with the April fair, and it lasts until the end of October. It is almost impossible to obtain tickets for the opening events; it is much easier later in the season, either just before the fight at the *Maestranza* gates, or through your hotel or at the Tourist Office. Tickets never cost less than $US 20, and often much more.

The cheapest are *gradas* (standing space only); *tendidos* (open seats) are more expensive, and *barreras* (covered gallery seats) are very expensive indeed.

Should you wish to visit one of the bull-farms, we suggest **El Rocío** (tel. 577-1212), at only 15 miles from Seville, where a guide will provide detailed information and, should you insist, even a small *corrida* of your own, where you may confront one of the more domesticated local bulls.

Soccer
According to many Sevillans, even the greatest controversies of Spanish history fade in comparison with the one and only really great conflict. And this is not the Andalusian-Catalonian dispute, nor the strife between orthodox and atheists. It is not the polemics between right and left, nor that of the supporters of United Europe against the Spanish Nationalists. All these fade and disappear when the two local soccer teams confront each other at the Seville Stadium: the *Real Betis Balompié* and the *Seville Club de Futbol*. Recently, however, this is a rather rare event, since the first team, whose most fervent fan is none other than the Prime Minister of Spain, has recently been relegated to the second Division...

The Spring Festivals
After a rather brief and generally very moderate winter, Seville is ready for the spring festivals. The first one is the *Semana Santa* (Holy Week) of Easter (*Pascua*). It is an almost uninterrupted sequence of religious processions, with the whole population streaming to the Great Cathedral from all the main quarters of the city. Then comes the *Feria de Abril*, a colourful regional fair frequented by local people, farmers from the whole province and thousands of tourists. The streets overflow with people, and there is not a single hotel bed available in the whole town.

The Semana Santa

The local clergy and their assistants will have toiled for several weeks before the event. When the time comes, it is an encompassing experience, a feast for one's eyes, ears and spirit. In the Middle Ages the participants used to wear a crown of thorns over their head, — a symbol of the Christ's Calvary. Today they wear a rather more comfortable but not less impressive peaked hat.

The tradition of the Holy Week processions dates from the year 1340, when a modest following of chosen believers marched from church to church behind a symbolic cross. The original processions were organized on the spur of the moment, without a fixed itinerary. Later the greater guilds took the matter in hand, and the processions became a meticulously organized competition, in which each of the guilds tried to show off its orthodoxy, its riches and its power. While today the original guilds have practically disappeared, the *hermandades* and *cofradías* have survived as social brotherhoods and extended-family groups.

In the 15th century a new invention was introduced: that of the *pasos* (mobile stages), bearing statues and effigies representing New Testament scenes — in Renaissance and Baroc styles. Each *paso* was accompanied by its own musical band playing the *saeta*, a flamenco-like beat that urged all followers to dance.

The tradition became a permanent fixture when, at the beginning of the 17th century, each *saeta* was assigned a fixed itinerary, starting from different neighbourhood churches but ending together at the Great Cathedral. Gradually the event took on the form it maintains to-day.

The week begins with a sequence of small, local, preparatory processions. Then, on *Jueves Santo* (Holy Thursday), everything clicks into high gear. In the early afternoon an endless column of women in black garb streams from the neighbourhood churches along the crowded streets of the centre of town. Things get even hotter on the *Viernes Santo* (Holy Friday). Already at sunrise the various *hermandades* and *cofradías* stream into their starting stations, to make their way toward Plaza de San Francisco. This is where one should stand (if only he can get up early enough to elbow himself in...) to really enjoy the sight.

Then, at the end, one should try to reach La Macarena, where the final ceremonies take place.

The April Fair

After a brief respite from the Holy Week fever, the Sevillans get ready for the *Feria de Abril*, which takes place during the last week of April, with lots of music, singing, dancing — and the biggest trade fair of the year in the whole of Andalusia. Traders and farmers, pickpockets and tourists, children of all ages leave their abodes and seem to be settled permanently along the main streets of Seville, to live and make merry.

In the Middle Ages, market days were very popular throughout Europe. In the 13th century King Alfonso X proclaimed that two fairs be annually held in Seville: the spring fair and the autumn fair. Somehow, over the years, the custom was forgotten, until Queen Isabella II renewed it in 1874.

Today the Fair is sponsored by traders, politicians and local leaders, and has gradually become one of the major Andalusian cultural and folkloristic events.

More than 1,000 stalls and tents (*casetas*) appear overnight side by side along most streets of the city, south of the Los Remedios quarter.

The fair starts coming to life around 1pm with a type of social event. The town notables ride about town on horseback and fancy carriages. Men and women turn out in their best clothing. At 3pm the occupants of all *casetas* sit down to a fabulous lunch. A brief siesta is then unavoidable, before taking off for the corridas, which take place at the Maestranza arena. The April *corridas* are the first of the season (tickets must be purchased weeks ahead...).

After the *corridas* things really get under way. At dusk all the *casetas* light up and fill up with passers by. Music and dancing, the courting of great *matadors* and other VIPs, and finally everybody sits down to a serious night of drinking, with more dancing and singing that last until sunrise.

The *casetas* are usually open to invited guests only; and the fair can be enjoyed in full only from a *caseta*; tourists unable to get themselves invited personally should register in time at the Tourist Office, where they will be able to purchase their own *caseta* seat.

The April Fair is a spontaneous popular festival, without fixed programmes and timetables. If you happen to be in Seville toward the end of April, do not miss it: it is a really unforgettable experience.

Christopher Columbus, the man behind the sailor

Columbus and the Old World

Even five centuries after his celebrated voyage, Columbus is still a figure of myth and mystery.

He was probably born in 1451 in Genoa, the son of a well known local silk trader. The origins of his family are not clear; Columbus himself sometimes signed his letters "Colón" (in Spanish), and sometimes in French: "Colomb". As is often the case with famous heroes of the past, there are several — not too well founded — national claims to his lineage.

Already at 15 young Christopher enrolled in Genoa's Merchant Navy, scouring the Mediterranean from East to West, and even reaching the shores of the Black Sea. In 1472 he had already become the captain of one of Philip d'Anjou's pirate ships. In 1476 his own pirate ship was sunk by one of Genoa's warships, and he was lucky to save his skin by swimming ashore to Portugal. In later years Columbus loved to recount this old adventure of his, claiming that his survival was granted him by God, who had such a glorious future in store for him...

Luckily Columbus happened to reach the Portuguese shores at the very gates of the *Sagres* school for sailors. Soon he settled into a life of leisure in Portugal, and had his two brothers Diego and Bartholomew join him from Genoa. Having established himself as a fully trained sea-captain, he married into one of Lisbon's best families, and his good connections got him the appointment of Royal Explorer of the Atlantic Ocean. In the course of these first travels of his, he is known to have reached the Western coasts of Africa at least once, (in what is probably known today as the Republic of Ghana); he also visited the British Islands, and, some claim, he even ventured as far as Iceland.

This was the age of discovery, with most European sailors involved in the dispute over Earth's spherical or flat shape. Hence the controversial efforts to reach the Indies, China and Japan from the west. Henry "the Navigator" was an enthusiastic supporter of such exploits, and even founded an institute dedicated to the planning and organization of similar sea ventures. Columbus himself fell under the spell of the "West Indies" dream, hoping to reach the mythical lands of Ophir and Tarshish of Biblical memory from the west. In his expeditions across the North Atlantic Ocean, he had learned to cope with the moods and perils of that great and stormy sea.

Toward the end of the 15th century South-Eastern Europe was in turmoil: its lands were threatened by a new wave of expansion by the Ottoman Empire, and the Spices Trail was not as secure as it had been in the past. The discovery of a new approach to India and China would have been very welcome indeed.

On the other side, almost the whole of the Iberian peninsula had been reconquered from the Moors, and Spain was entering its days of glory.

In the meanwhile Columbus was busily planning his great voyage westward; but when he submitted his proposal to King Joao II of Portugal, the King decided to reject it after several lengthy delays.

In 1485, disappointed by that rejection, Columbus crossed over to Spain, seeking new support for his ambitious expedition. For the next seven years he waited, busying himself with the study of the Bible (perhaps hoping to please his Most Christian Majesty). But he never relinquished his dream of discovery, and submitted again new proposals to the Spanish Court over and over. Finally he succeeded in winning the favour of Queen Isabella, and the date was set.

*I*NTRODUCTION

On 3 August 1492 Columbus sailed from Palos de la Frontera, (not far from Seville), on board the *Santa Maria* (a 110 feet "caravelle"), accompanied by two minor ships, the *Niña* and the *Pinta*. On 12 October 1492 his ships landed at what is known today as the isalnd of Santo Domingo.

Most sea historians believe that Columbus was not the first European to reach American shores. Today a Viking ship is known to have landed in Newfoundland as far back as the 10th century. However, settlement was not attempted on prior occasions. Columbus' expedition was specifically designed to create a permanent bridgehead on the western shore, that would be used as a base in following voyages. Columbus was also the first to leave a detailed scientific diary, destined to serve as a fundamental guide to all later explorers. The general consensus therefore, that Columbus was the "Discoverer of America", is justified.

Many Americans reject the term "Discovery of America" as a characteristic expression of European chauvinism, and would rather use a more symmetric term, such as "the Meeting of Two Worlds".

Columbus and the New World

Back from his first voyage, Columbus landed in Spain on 15 March 1493, having explored the coasts of Santo Domingo and of several other islands, known today as the Antilles. He still believed that he had reached the eastern coasts of India. His reports were received with such enthusiasm, that he was soon able to plan his second expedition with a fleet of no less than 17 ships. This fleet sailed on 25 September 1493, to return almost two years later, in June 1495. During this second expedition, he visited several other Caribbean islands and even attempted to settle some of them. However, Columbus' administrative talents were not up to his seamanship standards, and the new settlers soon became embittered and mutinous. His third expedition did not gain the clamorous support that he had expected, and Columbus set sail westward in 1498 with only six ships under his command. In this voyage he is known to have reached the continental coasts of Venezuela (South America) for

*I*NTRODUCTION

the first time. He returned from that voyage under irons, accused of having attempted to rob the crown of its new possessions in what he believed were the Eastern coasts of India.

Columbus was able to convince his Queen that he was innocent of the charge; he was released from prison and reinstated. In 1502 once again he sailed westward, reaching the coasts of Central America, from present day Honduras to Panama. On his return he was again imprisoned, and accused of high treason.

What really made Columbus tick no one really knows, even today. He died on 20 May, 1506 in Valladolid, shortly after once again being released from jail and reinstated. He never knew that he had "discovered America". Three years after his death his last wish was finally granted, and his remains were buried at the *Las Cuevas* monastery, near Seville, where he had spent some of his best years.

But his bones were not granted permanent rest. When the importance of his discoveries was officially recognized, his body was exhumed in 1536, to be reinterred in his own land of discovery, beyond the ocean. Finally, in 1544, after the inauguration of the new Santo Domingo Cathedral, his remains found their due resting place within that shrine.

For ever? No: in 1796, when Santo Domingo was about to become a French colony, once more Columbus' remains were transferred, this time to Santiago, the capital of Spanish Cuba.

But Spanish fortunes were on the ebb throughout the world. When Cuba was about to be lost, Columbus' bones, which had in the meanwhile been proclaimed a Spanish National Monument, were brought back to Seville, where they remain to this day, within the Great Cathedral. However, some historians claim that the body is not really the great sailor's remains. It may belong to his son, whose body was buried beside his father's in Santo Domingo; in that case, it would seem that Christopher Columbus' remains are still on that island...

Seville owes much of her Renaissance glory to Columbus' discovery. He lived at the *Las Cuevas* monastery for several years. His name is honoured not only at his Cathedral tomb, but also at the Archivo de Indias (where a large part of his personal library is preserved) and at the monastery he loved. A model of his *Santa Maria* caravelle is also preserved at the Archives.

America owes its name, as is well known, to a slightly later Italian explorer, Amerigo Vespucci, who was the first to recognize that the new lands were not the eastern coasts of India, but rather a New World. He also sailed from Seville (in 1499), landed in Venezuela and proceeded to explore the mouth of the Amazonas river. He was later appointed by the Spanish Crown head of the Sevillan New World Chamber of Commerce.

Was Columbus just an adventurer — or a man of high ideals? Was he dedicated to the idea of discovery? Or was he just another successful trader, who happened by chance to land his ships where he did? Was he a greedy conqueror, or a fanatic bigot? An opportunist or a despot? We shall probably never know his true motives; his real beliefs and his heart's desires will remain a mystery forever. Whatever may be the case, it must be recognized that in more than one way Columbus' discovery changed the face of the world — even if he was only one of a number of explorers and discoverers, his contribution to humanity cannot be over-estimated.

I*NTRODUCTION*

Part Two — Getting Ready to Go

When to come

Seville has three main tourist seasons. The peak season is undoubtedly spring (from mid-March to the beginning of May), with the *Semana Santa* (Easter) Festival and the *Feria de Abril*. The weather is fine (in the 70sF), and the sights spectacular. However, you will find the city appallingly overcrowded, excessively high-priced and amply "pickpocketed". And it is almost impossible to find good accommodation or to hire a car.

May is the right time for a quiet, satisfactory visit. The weather is not yet torrid, the land is green, April's crowds are but a memory, while the city recovers its strength. Summer (in more than one sense the "hot" season) has a certain appeal but presents also some problems. Air-conditioning is rare, even at many of the better hotels, and at temperatures well above the nineties (F) the siesta tends to last for most of the afternoon hours. September and October are slightly cooler, but then once again the city is swamped with tourists, and prices skyrocket again.

The winter (December-February) is the season preferred by Spanish tourists, who enjoy the weather — and the prices, which may plummet to half the peak season rates.

Holidays and Events

Andalusians are a fun-loving people; they love *fiestas* of all sorts:

1 January — New Year Day.

5-6 January — The Epiphany, celebrated along the banks of the Guadalquivir. A time of legends and of gifts, with decorated rafts anchored all along the river, announcing the coming of the Three Kings...

February — A three-day long Carnival, just before Ash Wednesday. Musical programmes at the *Lope de Vega* theatre in town. The main festival, however, is in Cadiz, and many tourists take the opportunity to see the sights and visit that town too.

28 February — *Dia de Andalucía* — a great regional holiday.

19 March — San José day, patron of Seville.

Easter Week — the famous Sevillan *Semana Santa*, with the whole population on its feet: processions, chorals, dancing, solemn Masses and scores of private parties. The peak is on *Jueves Santo* and on *Viernes Santo* (Holy Thursday and Friday), when offices, banks and shops are closed.

Last week in April — the *Feria de Abril* is a ten-day event of fairs and celebrations, with thousands of tourists and Spanish visitors from all over Andalusia and Extremadura.

1 May — *Dia del Trabajo* (Workers' Day); a national holiday.

May — Corpus Christi. A national holiday.

25 July — Santiago Apostolo, patron of Spain. A national holiday.

15 August — the day of the *Asuncion* of the Virgin Mary. A national holiday.

12 October — Columbus' Day. A national holiday.

1 November — *Todos los Santos* (All Saints). A national holiday.

6 December — *Dia de la Constitucíon Española* (Constitution Day). A national holiday.

8 December — *Inmaculada Concepcíon de la Virgen* (the Immaculate Conception); various religious festivals at the Cathedral and in other churches.

25 December — *La Navidad* (Christmas). This holiest of all Christian festivals is celebrated with carols, presents, solemn masses and the midnight mass; also with the greatest Andalusian horse fair and races.

Documents
Citizens of the USA and the European Community only need a valid passport if they are entering Spain for a

period of up to six months. Citizens of other countries should inquire at their travel agents before their departure. If a visa is required, your agent will be happy to assist.

You may be asked to show your return ticket to obtain a visa; the visa itself specifies its term (up to 180 days) and the number of authorized entries. This is important, especially if you plan to visit some other country, such as Portugal, for example, during your stay. If your visa permits just one entry, it will not be valid on your return from Portugal!

Car drivers must have an international permit (citizens of Europe may use their own driving license, but they may be asked for its Spanish translation).

The Students' International Card is recognized at most Sevillan sites, and its bearer will be entitled to substantial discounts. If you are eligible, bring your card with you. If you're under 24, you may be able to obtain a student card at home, even if you are not a university student.

Insurance
Don't ever travel abroad without a suitable insurance policy, covering medical expenses, loss of property, luggage and ticket refund. If you are carrying valuables, make it a point to have them included in your policy.

Customs
Tourists are allowed to bring any amount of foreign currency into Spain; sums amounting to more than 100,000ptas (Pesetas), or 500,000ptas in foreign currencies (about $US4,500) , in cash or in travelers' cheques, must be declared at the port of entry.

There are no dues to be paid for a maximum of 200 cigarettes, one litre of alcohol, 2 litres of wine and the usual personal effects; European citizens are allowed to import 300 cigarettes and up to 5 litres of wine. Antiquities, works of art and religious objects will be allowed to be taken out of the country only on presentation of specific permits.

How much will it cost
Seville is an aristocratic and expensive city. Hotels tend

to be considerably more expensive than in the rest of Spain, although during the winter you may find some very attractive offers.

The following are an indication of daily double occupancy prices, at the peak of the summer season:

High tourism — staying at one of the very best hotels and eating at the best restaurants will cost you a minumum of $US 450 — and for the splurgers it may come to substantially more.

Selective tourism — at 4-5 star hotels, with two daily meals at some of the best restaurants, plus the usual extras, will cost you $US 250-400 a day; for singles, $250.

Comfortable tourism — at one of the several 2-3 star hotels, with one impeccably good daily meal and all the extras you may need for evening entertainment, museums, etc., will cost you $US 150-250; $120 for singles.

Inexpensive tourism — Young people, backpacking their own sleeping bags, may be able to find in Seville inexpensive lodgings in the centre of town; such accommodation is almost never air-conditioned, and showers and toilets may have to be shared. But, eating at the simpler places or buying your own food at the supermarket you will manage comfortably with no more than $70 a day (40 for singles). However, remember that Seville is not the ideal place for this type of tourism.

(During Expo '92 all prices are liable to climb much, much higher...).

What to wear
Informal summer clothes are good for all seasons in Seville; sunglasses and a sun-hat are a must during the summer, together with all the gear needed at the swimming pool and at the tennis court. In winter you will do well to take some warm clothing and footwear.

Sevillans like sharp dressers and will show it; the local gentry is very much *á la mode* and makes it a point to wear the latest creations of high fashion. At business meetings, in the best hotels and restaurants, in church and at the theatre one has to keep up with the Joneses, even when the temperature soars to the 100°s(F).

*I*NTRODUCTION

Part Three — Easing the Shock: Where Have We Landed?

How to get there

By air

San Pablo, Seville's airport, is less than 8 miles east of town, on the Carmona Road. It services scores of daily *Iberia* flights as well as some regular flights from other airlines. The airport has been considerably improved and expanded for EXPO '92, to accommodate a number of flights similar to those of a regular international airport. For detailed information, call tel. 451-0677. However, San Pablo remains a facility of limited capability, and many flights will be landing at the neighbouring airports of Malaga and Jerez, which have also undergone extensive restoration works, and are connected to Seville by bus. The airport telephone number is tel. 451-6111.

From airport to town there are three alternative means of transportation:

By bus — the EA line leaves every hour for the centre of town (a 35 minute journey). The bus stops at the *Santa Justa* railway station and has its terminal at *Puerta de Jerez*, near the Central Tourist Office. The trip is comfortable and very cheap. During EXPO '92 several buses are added, and with more frequent rides, the traditional long and tiresome queues will probably be eliminated.

By taxi — Arriving tourists will generally find a long line of taxis, waiting for their fares outside the terminal. The ride to town costs about $15; it is a very comfortable and quick way to get there, but, of course, rather expensive.

By hired car — *Europcar*, *Avis*, *Hertz* and other agencies have their branches at the airport (see "Car hire agencies" below).

*I*NTRODUCTION

By rail
The Santa Justa railway station (*La Nueva Estación de Santa-Justa*) was inaugurated on 1991. It is very conveniently situated at about one mile from the centre of town; it includes a bank branch and a tourist information office, where one may inquire about available accommodation. Outside the station there is a large taxi stand — and the EA (to Puerta de Jerez) and 70 (to Prado de San Sebastian) bus stops. In the opposite direction the EA line will take you to the airport (Aeropuerto San Pablo).

Spanish rail services belong to the *RENFE*. The three best (and most expensive) lines are *Pendular*, *Talgo* and *Ter*. Beware of the so-called *Correo* (Postal) trains: they are slow, and stop at every station. The *Rapido* and *Express* trains do not live up to their names, but are neither too slow nor too expensive.

A new fast line has been inaugurated since April 1992 (also on the occasion of EXPO '92), connecting Seville with the capital, Madrid; its name is *AVE* and its trains run at a speed of more than 160 mph; tickets cost US$ 50-120.

For detailed information and timetables of the *RENFE*, call tel. 441-4111. Tickets may be purchased at the major travel agencies in town and at the *RENFE* office, near the Cathedral (Calle Zaragoza 29); for reservation of train seats, call tel. 442-1562.

There are several daily trains from Madrid (9-10 hours), Barcelona (14 hours), Cadiz (2 hours) and Cordoba (2 hours). There is also a Paris-Madrid-Seville line (24 hours).

All *Eurail Pass* and *Inter Rail* cumulative tickets are valid in Spain.

By bus
There is an extensive inter-urban bus network, connecting Seville with all major Andalusian centres. The most popular is the Cordoba line (*Alsima* buses, tel. 441-8811; every hour on the hour, $7 for the two hour trip).

The Seville-Lisbon line (*Julia* buses, tel. 422-4910, three weekly departures, $35 for the 9 hour ride through

Badajos). Tickets are available at most travel agencies and at the Plaza de San Sebastián terminal, not far east of the university.

For short rides in Andalusia buses are better than the railway; for longer rides (e.g. to Madrid or Barcelona), trains tend to be more convenient and more comfortable. The Andalusia bus terminal is also located at Plaza de San Sebastián (tel. 441-7111).

By car
Most Spanish throughfares are at least double-lane roads and comfortable. Petrol stations are frequent and there are many road-side restaurants along the mainroads. There is also a good toll-highway network.

The E-05 leaves Madrid southward and after about 330 miles reaches Seville, passing through Cordoba (90 miles north of the Andalusian capital). The E-05 does not end in Seville, but proceeds to Cadiz 70 miles away. The E-01 leads westward from Seville to Huelva (60 miles) and to the Portuguese border. The N-334 leads eastward to Malaga (130 miles) and Granada (150 miles).

Driving in Spain
Maximum highway speed is 75 mph (120 kmh); on other throughfares 55 mph (90 kmh) and in urban zones 35 mph (60 kmh). Motorbike riders (above 125 cc) are required to wear helmets. The *Guardia Civil de Trafico* (Road Patrol) is very strict, firm and uncompromising; fines are generally paid on the spot.

Petrol is sold as *Super* (97 octane), *Regular* (92 octane), and *Unleaded* (95 octane). Attendants expect to get a 50-100Ptas tip. The roads of Seville have been expanded and improved very recently, for the occasion of EXPO '92.

The road emergency telephone number is tel. 091.

Urban transportation
Seville is a relatively small town, and rather densely built. The easiest way to get around is by foot. Most of the interesting sites are close to one another, and several

zones (e.g. the Santa Cruz quarter and Sierpes St.) cannot be reached by motor vehicle. A leisurely walk is certainly the best way to get acquainted with the town and to appreciate its unique atmosphere.

Buses — The *TUSSAM Transportes Urbanos de Seville SA* provides a bus route covering the whole town; its orange buses run from 6am to midnight (Sundays and holidays from 7am). Some lines (called *líneas noctúrnas*) also run from midnight to 3am. The main bus terminal is on Plaza Nueva, near the City Hall. The *Archivio de Indias* stop is close to the pedestrian malls of the historic centre (where the Cathedral and the Alcázar are located).

The *Bonobus* card (available at most kiosks and bus stations) is convenient for multiple daily rides; there are also multiple-ride tickets on sale — 10 rides at a 40% discount.

TUSSAM — tel. 463-0681; lost-and-found objects on the bus, tel. 421-5694)

Horse-drawn cabs are a popular tourist treat in Seville. The cost of the ride (generally not more than 15 minutes) is to be bargained with the coachman. This used to be the means of transportation of the Sevillan aristocracy throughout the centuries. Excellent if and when one wants to give his/her legs a well earned rest. The cabs wait for their fares near the Alcázar, by the Maria Luisa Park and elsewhere.

Taxis — remain the unavoidable means for quick urban transportation. A supplement will be charged for hand-luggage, for longish waits and night fares (10pm-6am). A taxi ride to the airport or to the camping site is more expensive than the regular rates.

Radiotaxi: tel. 458-0000.
Teletaxi: tel. 462-2222.
Radio-Teléfono Taxi: tel. 435-9835.

Private or hired cars — this is possibly the worst means of transportation in town. However, it is also the best way to get to out-of-town sites. In Seville most streets and alleys are too narrow for motorized comfort; many are one-way-drives, and others are closed to motor-vehicles. The passable ones are almost chronically jammed.

Car-hire agencies

Most agencies offer discount rates for week-ends (Friday to Monday).

ATA: Almirante Lobo, Edificio Cristina, tel. 422-0958, 429-0957.

ATESA: 7 Plaza Carmen Benitez, corner of Calle Recaredo, tel. 441-9851, 441-9712 and 442-3450.

Autos Miguez: 13 Padre Marchena, tel. 421-6549 (nights), 421-2614 and 422-6334. Fax 451-4315.

Avis: 15b Ave. de la Constitucíon, tel. 422-1512 and 421-6549. Fax 421-5370. At the airport, tel. 451-4315.

Tavares: 17 Bécquer, tel. 437-3232, 437-1292 and 437-8727. Fax 437-3232.

Europcar: 32 Recaredo, tel. 441-9403, 441-9506 and 441-9505. Fax 442-5410.

Hertz: 3 Ave. Republica Argentina, tel. 427-8887 and 427-9388. Fax 427-6322. At the airport, tel. 451-4720.

ITAL: 9 Ave. Republica Argentina, tel. 427-7552 and 427-7551.

Hispalcar Rent-a-Car: 9 Ave. San Francisco Javier, Edificio Seville 2, tel. 465-0703 and 465-4807. Fax 465-9555.

Regente Car Rental: 1 Paseo de las Delícias, tel. 421-1858 and 421-2401.

Rentalauto S.A.: 3 Fernando IV, tel. 427-8184.

Seville Car S.A.: Almirante Lobo, Edificio Cristina, tel. 422-2587 and 422-4678. Fax 422-5595.

Tourist services

The Regional Administration of Andalusia (*Junta de Andalucia*) has tourist information stalls at the airport and at the railway station, where you may find maps and various interesting brochures. Hotel room reservations may be made at the hotels' union stall at the airport.

Multilingual information is available at the main tourist office, on Ave. de la Constitución, near the Archivo de Indias. The staff is well versed on all matters Andalusia, and Seville in particular. Open Monday-Friday, 9.30am-7.30pm, Saturday 9.30am-2pm, tel. 422-1404. The municipal Tourist Information Office is on Paseo de las Delícias, not far from the Puente del Generalísimo (tel. 423-4465); the staff may be able to help you find hotel accommodation.

Sevillan architecture

*I*NTRODUCTION

Accommodation

Many hotels reside in old mansions and palatial residences; the rooms are spacious and attractive, with lots of character but little air-conditioning. Stucco and *azulejo* are ever-present, together with plotted plants and shadowed courtyards. The staff is courteous, quick and efficient.

There are five classes of hotels and one super-de-luxe hotel, the *Alfonso XIII*, one of the best in Spain. Even some of the most modest establishments, however, may be sited in majestic old palaces, such as *La Rabida* (2-star) or *Simón* (1-star) for example.

At most 4 and 5-star hotels you can expect to find air-conditioned rooms (but even here, you may discover that air-conditioning is only turned on at the mid-day peak hours, to be turned off by mid-afternoon). Scores of smaller and cheaper hotels are in the Santa Cruz quarter. Most luxury establishments are between the Cathedral and the river.

The number of available hotel rooms does not meet the requirement, and as early as spring most hotels will be overbooked. Early reservations are simply a must — not only for spring, but for summer as well. In the suburbs there are some additional 800 rooms, used mostly by group-tours organizers and connected with the city by air-conditioned buses. On the occasion of EXPO '92 several new hotels have been opened, almost doubling the number of available rooms.

High standards and scarce availability are very bad news when we come to prices, and indeed you will find Sevillan hotels much more expensive than their counterparts in all major Spanish resorts elsewhere. Accommodation will almost certainly be the major item in your budget.

The prices indicated here refer to daily double-occupancy during the high-summer season, bed and breakfast only; they will be considerably lower in winter, but also much stiffer in spring.

5-star — US$ 250-300 per night.
4-star — US$ 150-270 per night.
3-star — US$ 90-150 per night.

2-star — US$ 60-100 per night.
1-star — US$ 40-80 per night.

5-Star Hotels
Alfonso XIII: 2 San Fernando, tel. 422-2850, fax 421-6033. The best in town, frequented by many VIPs. A tourist site on its own merit.
Príncipe de Astúrias: Isla de la Cartúja, tel. 429-2383 and 429-2222; fax 429-0428. Modern and elegant, near EXPO '92.
Tryp Colon: 1 Canaléhjas, tel. 422-2900, fax 422-0938. Recommended. Central and comfortably refurbished.
Andalusi Park: Benacazón (out of town), tel. 471-0651. A modern, outstanding establishment, with sport facilities and an artificial lake.

4-Star Hotels
Residéncia Doña Maria: 19 Don Remondo, tel. 422-4990, fax 422-9765. Excellent old-style residential hotel, very close to the historic centre. Relatively low-priced.
Grand Hotel Lar: 3 Plaza Carmen Benitez, tel. 441-0361, fax 441-0452. Very modern; recommended.
Inglatérra: 7 Plaza Nueva, tel. 422-4970, telex 72244. A simple front, but very pleasant interiors. Central.
Pasaréla: 11 Ave. de la Borbolla, tel. 441-5511, fax 442-0727. In one of the best residential areas, near the Maria Luisa Park.
Porta Coeli: 49 Ave. Eduardo Dato, tel. 457-0040, fax 457-8580. Large and modern.
Sol Lebréros: 2 Luis de Morales, tel. 457-9400, fax 458-2309. Off centre.
Sol Macaréna: 2 San Juan de Ribera, La Macarena quarter, tel.437-5800, fax 438-1803.
Melia Sevilla: 3 Ave. de la Borbolla, tel. 442-2611, fax 442-1608. Quiet and modern, near the Maria Luisa Park. Recommended.
Husa Sevilla: 90 Pagés del Corro, Triana, tel. 434-2412, fax 434-2707. Far from the town centre, past the river. Recommended for quiet, longer stays.
Las Casas de la Judería: Callejon de Dos Hermanas, Plaza Sta. Maria la Blanca, tel. 422-8776 and 441-5150. A very attractive residential hotel in the Santa Cruz quarter. Recommended.
Parador Nacional Alcázar del Rey Don Pedro: Carmona, 20 miles from Seville, tel. 414-1010, fax 414-1712.

3-Star Hotels

Alcázar: 10 Ave. Menéndez Pelayo, tel. 441-2011. Near the San Bernardo station and the Murillo Gardens. Recommended.

América: Plaza del Duque, tel. 422-0951, fax 422-4765. Modern and attractive, near a large shopping centre. Recommended.

Bécquer: 4 Reyes Católicos, tel. 422-2172 and 422-8900, fax 421-4400. A modest front, comfortable interiors and excellent service.

Corregidór: 17 Morgado, tel. 438-4238 and 438-5111, fax 437-6102. Pleasant Andalusian setting. Recommended.

Don Paco: 4-5 Plaza Padre Jerónimo de Córdoba, tel. 422-4931, fax 422-2824. central.

Residencia Fernando III: 21 San José, tel. 421-7708 and 421-7307. Within the historic centre.

Giralda Playa: 3 Calle Sierra Nevada, tel. 441-6661, fax 441-9352.

Residencia Monte Carmelo: 7 Calle Turia, tel. 427-9000. Refreshingly quiet, in Los Remedios quarter, past the river. Outstanding service. Recommended.

Monte Triana: 24 Clara de Jesus Montero, tel. 434-3111, fax 434-3328. Near EXPO '92.

Residencia Venecia: 31-33 Trajano, tel. 438-1161. A small, friendly hotel. Recommended.

Virgen de los Reyes: 129 ave. Luis Montoto, tel. 457-6610, fax 457-6815. In a new, modern neighbourhood. Not far from the Santa Justa railway station.

Reyes Católicos: 57 Gravina, tel. 421-1200. Relaxing atmosphere, not far from the Fine Arts Museum, recommended.

Oromana: Ave. de Portugal, Alcala de Guadaira, 10 miles from town, tel (95)470-0804. Countryside atmosphere.

1-2-Star Hotels

Montecarlo: 51 Gravina, tel. 421-7501. Quiet, but relatively high-priced. Not far from the Fine Arts Museum.

Residencia Ducal: 19 Plaza de Encarnación, tel. 421-5105. Central, but noisy. Ask to see your room before you check in.

Internacionál: 17 Aguilas, tel. 421-3207. Near Santa Cruz; beautiful scenery.

Puerta de Triana: 5 Reyes Católicos, tel. 421-5404, fax 421-5401. Comfortable, near the Maestranza arena.

La Rábida: 24 Calle Calestar, tel. 422-0960. A charming

At the bull-ring

hotel in a pleasant setting; near the Cathedral. Recommended.

Residencia Murillo: 7-9 Lope de Rueda, tel. 421-6095. Traditional Sevillan atmosphere in Santa Cruz. Recommended.

Residencia Sevilla: 5 Daoiz, tel. 438-4161. A small hotel near Sierpes St., in a restored old patrician residence. Recommended.

Simón: 19 García de Vinuesa, tel. 422-6669 and 422-6660. Central and quiet, but relatively high-priced.

Zaida: 26 San Roque, tel. 421-1138. Rooms of various standards, priced accordingly.

Hostels and pensions

Backpackers and other frugal tourists will be glad to hear about simple, lower-priced accommodation. There are scores of private residences whose rooms are rented by the day or by the week. Most rooms are very simple, basically furnished with beds, tables, some storing place and a water-faucet. Toilets and showers are generally to be shared with the occupants of other rooms on the same floor. You are strongly advised not to check in before viewing the room; eventually, you may inquire about an alternative setting. Pensions are classified according to their services, from 1 to 3-stars, but even 3-stars do not imply adequate comfort.

Most pensions are found on Seville's side streets and alleys. The most popular cheap accommodation neighbourhood is Santa Cruz, where you may stroll around, looking for something affordably suitable. Don't be ashamed to bargain (unless you are really frantic...). A 1-star double room will cost you US$ 20-40 per night — and only a little less than that for singles. You may be able to get a discount for multiple night occupancy.

Between April and August early reservations by phone are strongly recommended.

Do not leave unguarded valuables in your room.

Seville has one *Albérgue Juvenil* (youth hostel); the telephone number is tel. 461-3150. The address is 2 Isaac Peral — but don't even look for it unless you have reserved a room!

*I*NTRODUCTION

Camping

Tent or trailer accommodation is available, not far from town, at the following sites:

Cámping Sevilla: 6 miles off town, toward the airport. Open all year, and very good.
Club de campo: 13 Ave. da la Libertad, on the road to Dos Hermanas. Open all year.
Villsom: 5 miles from town on the road to Cadiz. Closed December and January.

General Information

Currency

The Spanish currency is the *Peseta* (in short pta.) Like most European currencies, it is very stable, with slight daily variations according to international money market trends. Banknotes in circulation are worth 500, 1000, 2000, 5000 and 10,000 ptas, and small change coins are worth 1, 5, 10, 25, 50, 100, 200 and 500 ptas.

Money changing is bank business; look for the *Cambio* notice at the entrance of bank branches; the larger banks, such as the *Banco Popular Español* or the *Banco de Bilbao*, will probably offer slightly better rates of exchange.

Beware: the money changing fees charged by Spanish banks are among the highest in Europe. It is generally more convenient to change lump sums of a single currency, this way you will not be charged for more than one transaction. Even better, try to come well supplied with pesetas from abroad.

Winter banking hours are Monday-Friday 9am-2pm; Saturday 9am-1pm. In summer banks are closed on Saturday, and on weekdays close at 1pm. On holidays and weekends all banks are closed. A single branch, in Avenída da la Constitución, is open for exchange on workdays until 4.30pm. Hotels and travel agencies will also accept foreign currencies and change them into pesetas. — but at considerably lower rates.

Credit cards are welcome in all hotels and travel agencies,

*I*NTRODUCTION

La Giralda — Seville's famous spot

and also in many restaurants. In small businesses they are generally frowned upon; they mostly accept local currency.

Shopping Hours

Siesta hours are rigidly observed all over Andalusia. Everybody locks up and hurries home, hoping to find some shelter from the torrid heat. In summer the entire town comes to a stand-still between 1 to 5pm; in winter there are some who dare reappear one hour earlier. The only activities that are pursued uninterruptedly are dining and resting, if possible in air-conditioned areas. And at least during the summer, the foolhardy might incur serious risks of dehydration; be warned!

Serving hours in restaurants are generally as follows:

Breakfast — 8.30-10am; **Lunch** — 12am-3pm and **Dinner** — 8pm-Midnight. Between meals most restaurants are closed.

Shops open at 9am, close for their *siesta* at 1pm or at most 1.30pm reopening at 5pm in summer and 4pm in winter. Saturday mornings only; Sunday and holidays closed.

Seville — a facade

Air-conditioned department stores, such as *El Corte Inglés*, are open for business all day long.

Public Offices are open Monday-Friday, 8am-3pm.

Communications
The Central Post Office is at 32 Ave. de la Constitución (Monday-Friday, 9am-1pm).

Stamps (*sellos*) are available at postal branches (*Correo*) and kiosks (*Tabacos*). Mail boxes marked *Extranjero* (abroad) are for mailing your letters home. Stamp collectors will find on sale, at a special counter of the Central Post Office marked *Filatélico*, a good selection of national stamps and commemorative envelopes.

Telephones — most public phones accept international calls; at night there is a discounted tariff from 10pm to 8am. Public phones are still coin-operated; for an international call you will better come prepared with a pocketful of 50 and 100ptas coins; the prefix for international calls is 07, followed by the target country's code and the regional code (without its "0") and finally the destination number. For information, dial 003. International calls may also be made from most hotels, but their overcharge is generally very high.

Telegrammes (*telegrámas*) may be phoned in (tel. 422-2200 for Spanish destinations, and tel. 422-6860 abroad), or sent off at all postal branches. Night telegrammes (*Telegráma de noche*) are cheaper than the day variety (but they will be sent off only the morning after).

The **Poste Restante** is at the Central Post Office (*Correo Central*). The address is 32 Ave. de la Constitución, Seville 41004 Spain.

Dailies in English, French and German are on sale at the best hotels and at several Ave. de la Constitución kiosks. They generally reach Seville in less than 24 hours.

Personal Security
Seville is dubiously famous for being the pickpockets' capital of Spain.

This pickpockets' epidemic is at least partly due to the exceedingly high unemployment prevalent throughout Andalusia. The peak season for picking pockets coincides, of course, with the high season of tourism, when the overcrowded streets provide an excellent arena for this internationally practiced and profitable sport.

Hard street violence in Seville, however, is much less than in most urban centres in Europe and in the Americas.

Young women travelling alone may sometimes be

molested, specially if they try to thumb a ride from town to town or if they wander around at night in certain urban areas.

Perhaps the highest risk is that of dehydration. Keep your head sheltered from the sun, and drink large quantities of (mineral) water. Should you experience even the slightest symptoms, medical care is immediately required. Beware of sunburns, equip yourself with a good reserve of suntan oil — and use your sunglasses during the sunny hours.

Photography

Your camera will probably be kept busy in Seville. Films are available in most gift shops along the Ave. de la Constitución, and they are not too expensive. We strongly recommend a selection of films with low ASA, suitable for the brilliant sunlight and the bright colours of Sevillan streets and sites.

Time; Electric current

The time zone of Spain is GMT + 1. Spanish summertime begins on the first Sunday of March and ends on the last Sunday of September. The change is widely and repeatedly advertised on the radio, TV and the daily press.

Like in all Europe, electric current is 220 V.

S EVILLE

Meet Seville

The Alfonso XII waterway, an arm of the Guadalquivir river, cuts through Seville from North to South. South-east of the San Telmo Bridge (Puente de San Telmo) is the old city. Over the centuries Seville grew from a farmers' and traders' hamlet into a Roman garrison town, then to a Moorish capital and finally, to the city you are going to meet. This is the *Centro*, the heart of Seville.

In the very middle of this *Centro* is the Plaza del Triunfo, a small square surrounded by some of Seville's grandest buildings. On one side you will see the Great Gothic Cathedral and its famous Giralda Belltower; on the opposite side stands the Alcázar, seat and residence of ancient Sevillan potentates. The Avenida de la Constitución, the main central artery of Seville, runs from north to south along the western side of the Cathedral. On this avenue you will find the central post office, the tourist information office, several bank branches and scores of gift shops.

At the northern end of the avenue stands the Ayuntamiento (City Hall). Here you will find also some department stores (such as the *El Corte Inglés*) and many of the best shops in town. East of the Plaza del Triunfo are some of the most interesting palaces in Seville and the Barrio Santa Cruz, always overflowing with strolling tourists. There are several quaint pubs and restaurants in this quarter, as well as many small pensions and rooms for rent.

Between the Avenida da la Constitución and the river is the Plaza de Toros de la Maestranza, one of the most renowned *corrida* arenas in Spain. This is the El Arenal neighbourhood, with many interesting sites, including the famous San Juan Hospital and the Torre del Oro (Golden Tower).

The great Maria Luisa Park, Seville's largest park, is further south, on the east bank of the Guadalquivir, surrounded on three sides by many interesting monuments and palaces.

The downtown centre we have briefly described covers a relatively small area and contains scores of interesting sites; it is therefore most suitable for a first walking tour. The railway station (Estación de Santa Justa) is not too far away, and the Triana historic popular quarter is just opposite, on the other bank of Alfonso XIII Waterway. EXPO '92 occupies a large section of La Cartuja Island, enclosed by the waterway and the river.

SEVILLE

A First Encounter with the City

Seville is an endless hoard of natural and architectural gems, and we believe it is very important to carefully plan one's first encounter with the city. Seville is so small that, if you can avoid getting swamped by the multitudes of sites, palaces and names, in a single first tour you will be able to plan your next steps.

The *Serva-Tours* Agency (39 García de Vinuesa, tel. 422-7414) offers some good brief (three hours) morning, afternoon and night tours of the city. Prices start from $US25 for adults, half-price for children aged 3-8. Shorter (one hour) river cruises start several times a day from the Torre del Oro pier; from the river you will enjoy a breathtaking view of the city. For information and reservations, call *Cruceros del Sur* (tel. 421-1392) or *Barco Lola* (tel. 462-7448).

You may also hire your own private guide (in English or in other languages) at the *ITA* (tel. 421-3894) or at *Guidetour* (tel. 422-2374). While it is more expensive than the standard group tours, you will have the advantage of setting your own pace and timetable.

Index
1. The Cathedral
2. The Alcázar
3. Santa Cruz Quarter
4. City Hall
5. Casa de Pilatos
6. Santa Justa train station
7. La Macarena
8. Alameda de Hércules
9. Fine Arts Museum
10. University of Seville
11. Bus Terminal
12. Maria Luisa Park
13. Plaza de España
14. La Maestranza bull ring
15. Torre del Oro
16. Triana
17. Los Remedios

SEVILLE

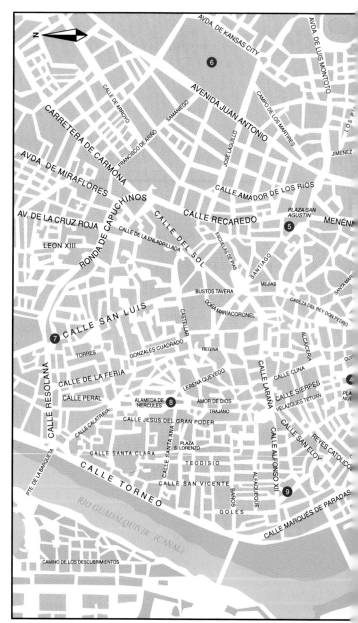

SEVILLE

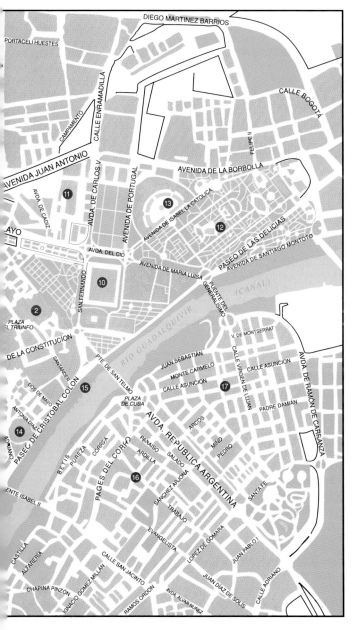

The Cathedral and the Alcázar — The Cross and the Crown

The two major forces of Sevillan life have been confronting one another for centuries from opposite sides of the **Plaza del Triunfo**: the Alcázar and the Cathedral. One of the largest churches in the world (and the largest Gothic monument of its type on Earth), the cathedral contains a hoard of priceless works of art. Its bell tower (La Giralda) dominates Seville's skyline and has become one of the symbols of the city.

The palace that forms the south-western border of the square is the Archivo de Indias, a museum of past Spanish colonial triumphs. The obelisk you will see in the middle of the square commemorates the great earthquake of 1755, which left Seville in ruins — and the reconstruction of the city soon after that disaster.

Almost all urban bus lines reach the Avenida de la Constitución, and the Archivo de Indias stop is a very good starting point for your tour.

The Cathedral
Leave the Plaza del Triunfo along the Fray Ceferino Gonzales Alley, toward the southern entrance of the cathedral and the Archivo de Indias.

The Cathedral is open to visitors on weekdays 11am-6pm, Saturdays 11am-5pm, Sundays and holidays 2-4pm. Entrance fee; tickets may be purchased up to one hour before closing time. The Cathedral is closed to visitors on Solemn Mass days: New Year Day, 6 January, 30 May, 15 August, 8 December and Christmas. Religious events and daily masses are held throughout the year.

Like many other Spanish churches, the Cathedral was built on a former mosque. In 1171 Caliph Abu Yacub Yusuf instructed his architect Ahmed Ibn Basu to build, a new Mosque, worthy of his glorious name, on the foundations of a much earlier Visigoth church. Ten years later Ibn

Basu presented his Caliph with his new creation: the grand Alhama Mosque, surrounded by a newly planted citrus grove. Two years later Ibn Basu also built its impressive minaret. The call of the *muezzin* called the faithful Moslem Sevillans to their devotions from the new minaret for less than a century: in the mid-13th century the Christian *Reconquistadores*, under King Ferdinand "The Saint", conquered Seville. The mosque was transformed into a church, and the minaret became its bell tower. The church was severely damaged by a 1366 earthquake, and remained in ruins for several decades.

In 1401 the City Council of the Elders undertook the building of a new great cathedral on the ruins of the *Alhama Mosque*. It was decided to spare no expense, and to build "such a church that all those who see it will think we are out of our minds". Actual construction began in 1402. No one knows who drew the cathedral's designs, because all the original drawings and documents were destroyed by fire centuries ago. However, the new cathedral was inaugurated with great pomp and ceremony in 1506, more than a hundred years after the cornerstone had been laid. According to some chronicles, the original designs were the works of Alfonso Martinez; according to the same sources, for more than a century the Cathedral was the largest in the whole world; it still is, to this day, the largest Gothic church in Europe. The Cathedral had to be restored several times over the centuries, but it is believed that the original design has always been successfully preserved.

Above the southern entrance (the visitors' entrance, known as **Puerta de San Crislóbal**), you will see some very beautiful Gothic decorations and bas-reliefs. In the dark passageway there is a sculpture by Arturo Mélida, illustrating the funeral of Christopher Columbus (Cristóbal Colón in Spanish). Four barons in full ceremonial garb bear the great explorer's coffin on their shoulders. (Re: Columbus' life and death, see "Columbus — the man behind the sailor").

In Arturo Mélidas' 19th century work, the pallbearers represent the four victorious Christian kings who delivered Spain from the Moors: the Kings of León, Aragon, Castilla and Navarra. Each of the figures holds a shield in his

THE CATHEDRAL

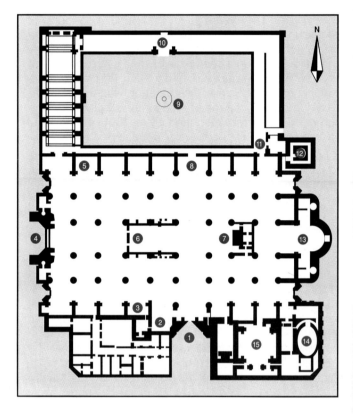

Index

1. Puerta de San Cristóbal
2. Capilla de Nuestra Señora de la Antigua
3. Capilla de San Hermenegildo
4. The main entrance
5. Capilla de San Antonio
6. The chorus wing
7. Capilla Mayor
8. Puerta de la Concepción
9. Patio de los Naranjos
10. Puerta del Perdón
11. Puerta del Lagarto
12. The Giralda
13. Capilla Real
14. Sala Capitular
15. Sacristía Mayor

Gothic style of the Cathedral

"The funeral of Christopher Columbus"

hands, decorated with the coat of arms of his kingdom. The coat of arms of Seville can be seen on the coffin itself.

This beautiful entrance leads you into the wide, shadowy spaces of the great Cathedral. It is simply enormous. Its floor space is more than 100,000 square feet; its ceiling is 180 feet high. The simplicity of its interior emphasizes its gigantic size and enhances the free flow of light and space within. One cannot avoid feeling awe-struck.

Turn left from the southern entry, toward the row of chapels along the wall. The first is the **Capilla de Nuestra Señora de la Antigua** (situated where the *Mihrab* — pulpit — used to stand in the old Mosque). According to an old legend, the Virgin Mary appeared twice on this spot: the first time to comfort the faithful, harassed by their Moslem rulers, and the second to praise King Fernando, who had delivered the town from the infidels. Several Archbishops are buried along the chapel walls.

The most impressive mausoleum is inside the second chapel, the **Capilla de San Hermenegildo**, where the tombs of Archbishop Juan de Cervantes and of Admiral Juan Mathé de Luna, are found. The latter died in the 14th century, and his remains were entombed here three centuries later.

Proceed along the chapel row to the main entrance. Clearly these great doors have remained closed for a very long time. This entrance was exclusively used by royalty. Before the crowning of Juan Carlos, Spain had no king for almost half a century — and the doors had never been opened during that time. In 1976, when King Juan Carlos paid his first royal visit, all Seville waited for the traditional reopening of the main cathedral entrance. But the saying that he was only a simple mortal, turned away, making his entrance through the southern doors used by all visitors.

When Pope John Paul II visited Seville, the main entrance was prepared once again. But having heard of King Juan's act, the Pope said bluntly that if the southern entrance was good enough for the King of Spain, it was certainly good enough for him. And that was it.

*S*EVILLE

Proceed now to the north-western corner of the cathedral. Here you will see a monumental iron statue of a woman. It is a perfect copy of the one set on the bell tower, to whom the tower owes its name: Giralda (windvane). Since the original cannot be seen from the tower itself, a visible copy was installed here.

The chapel you see on your right is the **Capilla de San Antonio**, with one of Murillo's best works on show above Pineda's beautiful altar. It represents, of course, the Saint. Murillo painted it in 1656, and sold it to the church for an enormous sum. Two centuries later, in 1875, the painting was stolen, and Saint Anthony's image was cut out and disfigured. The painting was recovered several months later in New York, and after its restoration it was reinstated in its original niche.

The **chorus** wing and the great chapel occupy the heart of the cathedral. The ebony chorus wing is richly engraved, and the small alabaster alcoves were used by visiting royalty and high gentry.

The main altar faces the great chorus of the **Capilla Mayor** (The Great Chapel). Try to elbow your way through the crowd to its protective balustrade, and admire the details of the gold-plated ebony reliefs of the main altar, whose 45 panels depict New Testament scenes. This altar, the largest in Spain, is one of the best examples of Gothic sculpture in Europe. The reliefs are the work of Pyeter Duncart, who worked at them for the last ten years of his life. After his death, in 1492, his pupils completed the altar according to the master's designs, and the masterpiece was finally completed in 1526. The balustrade itself is a beautiful Renaissance work. Don't miss the main chapel, even if you must fight your way to reach it.

On the Northern wall of the Cathedral you will see the **Puerta de la Concepción**. Across the door is a pleasant and refreshing courtyard. This is the **Patio de los Naranjos** (Yard of the Orange Trees), which used to serve as the main entrance to the old *Alhama Mosque*; it is through this yard that the followers enter. The contrast between the modest orange trees and the majestic structure of the cathedral is overwhelming. The courtyard

The glorious Giralda

The Royal Chapel

SEVILLE

A view from the Giralda

fountain was once used for the Moslem feet-cleaning ritual, before entering the mosque. Two popular heroes of the Spanish rebellion, put to death by the French in 1811, are buried in this courtyard.

The outside door of the courtyard, the **Puerta del Perdón**, is the main outer door used today by the believers.

Re-enter the Cathedral through the **Puerta del Lagarto** ("The Lizard's Gate"). Look at the stone engraving symbolizing the four main virtues of the Middle Ages: prudence (the lizard), strength (the elephant tusk), patience (the horse bit) and obedience (the scepter of Justice).

Outside the gate, turn left (eastward) to the **Giralda**, the pride of all Sevillans. The Cathedral bell tower, was originaly built toward the end of the 12th century, as the minaret of the Alhama Mosque.

The builders of the tower thought to make it easier for the climbers, and instead of a staircase you will find a climbing path, that after 35 right-angle turns will take you to the top, more than 300 feet above street level. La Giralda is topped by the great bronze windvane that gave it its name. The windvane (1568) is the work of the sculptor Bartolomé Morel, and it is in the shape of a beautiful young woman. Under the statue, beneath the roof, are 25 bells, whose toll is heard every hour on the hour throughout Seville.

From the top of the Giralda the view is fantastic. Seen from above, the roof of the cathedral seems to be supported only by its peripheral exterior arches, characteristic of the Gothic style; this effect, far from being illusory, reflects perhaps the main Gothic structural architectural element. Having paid your entrance fee at the cathedral, there is no additional fee to be paid for the climb up the Giralda.

Re-enter the Cathedral. Turn left (southward) to the **Capilla Real** (Royal Chapel). This chapel was reserved exclusively for the royal family. Its dimensions are indeed majestic, but its Baroc style is over decorated to be really impressive. What overwhelms the visitor is its size: 90 feet tall, 90 feet long, and 50 feet wide, it is probably bigger on its own than many full-fledged churches... Under the chapel is an ancient crypt, that probably belonged to the former Visigoth church. The builders of the cathedral left this ancient burial crypt untouched: Inside the crypt itself several Spanish kings are burried, including Ferdinand the Saint, who delivered Seville from the Moors, his wife Beatriz, and his son Alfonso XIII, "The Wise". The inscription on Ferdinand's tomb is in four languages: Spanish, Latin, Arabic and Hebrew.

At the south-eastern corner of the cathedral are two wide halls: the **Sala Capitular** (assembly hall) and the **Sacristía Mayor** (main vestry). Both are richly decorated with paintings and sculptures of various periods, from the 13th to the 18th century. Specially notable are Murillo's paintings, above the marble walls of the assembly hall, and the Tablas Alfonsinas, a beautiful 13th century Triptych dedicated to St. Theresa. Turn left from the Vestry, and leave the cathedral through the southern gate.

The Alcázar
The south-eastern side of the Plaza del Triunfo is occupied

by the **Alcázares Reales** — the Royal Residences, used over the centuries, probably since Roman times, by the rulers of Seville. It is one of the most famous and most beautiful buildings in Spain, well worth a special visit. At least 2-3 hours are required, and therefore you should plan your time according to the palace's opening hours: Monday-Saturaday, 9-12.45am and 3-5.30pm; Sunday 9-12.45am only. Entrance fee. The palace is closed to visitors when the royal apartments are occupied by the royal family.

Here, on the river bank, the Romans built the main stronghold of their new town, the Julia Romulea of Caesarian memory. Seville grew around this spot, century after century.

On their arrival, in the 8th century, the Moslems were frequently harassed by local tribes and, in the 9th century, also by Norman incursions. Abed-el-Rahman II had the building transformed into a fortified castle. In fact its name is but a corruption of the Arabic *Al Qasr* (The Castle); later the word "Alcázar" became a common term for the fortified castles also built in many other towns. The original components of the Moslem castle, however, have disappeared over the centuries.

At the beginning of the 11th century, the Cordoba Caliphate began to disintegrate, breaking down into a number of *taifas*. Seville was ruled independently by the Al Mutamid dynasty, who made of it the richest and most powerful taifa in Spain. A new princely residence was erected near the old castle, and named Alcázar Al Mubarak. Later, the new palace gradually grew, into today's Alcázar.

For two centuries the new palace was the residence of the Moslem rulers of Seville. Its splendour was such, that its fame was known beyond the borders of the Sevillan taifa. It became a world-renowned centre of science, arts and letters; it was praised by many a poet in several different languages: Arabic, Latin, Spanish and Hebrew. Its guests lived a life of leisure and comfort; it was an ivory tower of arts, science and culture.

After the Christian *Reconquista* the palace was often used by royalty. Ferdinand III, and his successor and

DON PEDRO PALACE

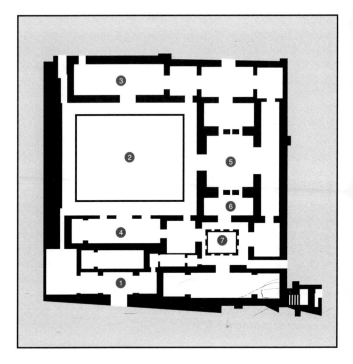

Index
1. Vestíbulo
2. Patio de las Doncellas
3. Salón de Carlos V
4. Dormitorio de los Reyes Moros
5. Salón de Embajadores
6. Sala de Felipe II
7. Patio de las Muñecas

son Alfonso "The Wise", reigned and died here. For Don Pedro I the palace was too small, so he built the Alcázar Nuevo at its side, as a symbol of his wealth and of Spain's power. When Philip II took up residence in Madrid, his new Capital, the Alcázar continued to serve as a royal residence.

SEVILLE

The entrance gate to the palace is on *Plaza del Triunfo*, where the horse drawn coaches wait for their tourist fares. Above the gate, the arch is covered with beautiful *azulejo* tiles, representing a crowned lion and a cross, symbolizing the victory of the Christian arms against the Moors. The *azulejos* gave the gate its name: **Puerta del Leon**. Inevitably, the image also gave rise to a legend, that in older times the gate was indeed guarded by wild lions, and that the name of the gate is in fact due not to its *azulejos* but to real lions.

Go through the entrance court, and you will come to the **Patio de la Montería** (Court of the Hunt), a characteristic Moorish style courtyard, whose arches, decorated with statues of kings, reveal the later contribution of *Reconquista* times. On the right side you will see the **Casa de la Contratación de Indias**, the Chamber of Commerce established by Queen Isabella "The Catholic". It served as a centre of trade with the "New World" colonies, from which she would firmly hold what already had become one of the main sources of Spain's riches. Here you will visit the **Cuarto del Almirante** (Admiral Hall), whose walls are covered with portraits of Spain's most famous admirals and sailors. The showpiece is a model of Columbus' caravelle, the Santa Maria. The next hall is the **Sala de las Audiencias** (Audience Hall), where the Queen graciously received the discoverer of America, who had safely returned from his second voyage. The paintings in this hall date from the 16th and 17th centuries.

Proceed now beyond these two beautiful halls, toward the majestic front of the great **Palacio del Rey Don Pedro**.

It is probably the grandest and most spectacular living example of *Mudéjar* architecture. The Moorish influence is still clearly evident; in fact the architects and builders of the palace were Moors, provided by the rulers of Granada and Toledo in homage to the King. The same mixture of Christian and Moslem themes are also recognized in the interior. The residential apartments are not too regal, but they are spacious and sunny, attractively pleasant.

You will clearly recognize the official splendour of much grander reception halls and audience rooms in other parts of the palace.

Turn left to the **Vestíbulo** (Main Hall). Through its corridors, you will reach the charming **Patio de las Doncellas** (Court of the Virgins), framed within a richly decorated portico, supported by exquisite marble columns. This is the heart of the ceremonial quarters of the palace.

The ethereal appearance of the courtyard columns is characteristic of the Moorish style, which abhorred the blunt expression of power characteristic of the massive stone Gothic pillars. The lacy ornamental stuccos of the walls add to the image of delicate fragility evoked by this charming courtyard.

The arches, doorways and windows of the courtyard are covered with breathtakingly beautiful coloured tiles. The true character of the town reveals itself here: the unique harmony born of the interlacing of two great cultures. The ground floor echoes the delicate spirit of the Moorish period, while the upper floor resonates with classical beauty. The columns and arches are clearly oriental; but the capitals are in the purest Ionic style.

The courtyard owes its name to the Christian virgins offered year after year in tribute to the Moslem rulers of Seville, who employed them as servants — or in other, more stimulating functions.

The Virgins' Courtyard leads to three large halls: the **Salón de Carlos V**, that owes its name to the beautiful ceiling commissioned by that Monarch; the **Salón de Embajadores** (Ambassadors' Hall), and the **Salón de la Media Naranja**. Here the King received his most important guests; along the walls of this hall are the effigies of 56 Kings of Spain, from Visigoth King Recaredus to Philip II of Habsburg.

Observe its entrance doors, so finely carved by the best Moslem woodcarvers in Toledo, to honour the great Christian King Don Pedro in Allah's Name... Its beautiful golden dome is the work of Diego Ruíz (1427).

The elongated rectangular **Sala de Felipe II** leads to the great **Sala de los Reyes Católicos** and to the **Patio de las Muñecas** (Court of the Dolls), in the heart of the royal apartments.

The royal family lived in the upper galleries that surround

the *Court of the Dolls*. The court's name is probably due to two effigies, inserted tongue-in-cheek by one of the builders. They are inserted into the right hand corner of the column coming from the Ambassadors' Hall. The entrance to the hall was absolutely forbidden, except for the king's family and his guests. Here Don Pedro murdered his half-brother Don Fadrique, who had made an unsuccessful attempt to dethrone the King, together with his twin brother. After his failure, Fadrique repented, and was readmitted to the palace. But Don Pedro, who had no confidence in the good faith of his two half-brothers, had him killed in 1358. Abu Said, a rich diamond merchant, was also put to death here by Don Pedro, who was greedy to put his hands on the merchant's priceless collection of precious stones. Abu Said was summarily disposed of, and the diamonds found their way to the Crown treasury... One of these diamonds, finally found its way to England, and to the British Royal Crown.

The royal apartments, with their pleasant living spaces, music rooms and bedrooms, are still used frequently by the royal family, and are therefore generally closed to the public. .

Now leave Don Pedro's Palace, and return to the *Patio de la Montería*. Follow the outer walls of the palace to the beautiful **Patio del Crucero** (Court of the Cross), a stylized garden divided in four sections by a median gallery — to which the garden owes its name.

This was the palace's private garden, site of the **Baño de Doña María de Padilla** (Donna Maria's Baths). That lady was a very popular concubine of Don Pedro's, and it was believed that those who drank from her bath would guarantee her favours. Beyond the courtyard you will come to the **Salones de Carlos V**, an 18th century wing built by Sebastian van der Borsch, who also built the large tobacco plant that later became the seat of the University of Seville.

The Alcázar Gardens
After the palace, you should visit also the **Alcázar Gardens** (Jardines de Alcázar). Here too you will

Don Pedro Palace — a Patio

SEVILLE

At the Alcázar Gardens

recognize the two main styles of Seville, the Moorish and the European, although here they are separated by a stone wall.

First you will come to a goldfish pool. Follow its side and take a stroll through the Moorish garden: its maze-like structure is intended to hide the outside world from the visitor's eyes, while the aromas of its herbs cover the smells of daily life. The fountain's water jets drown all foreign noises, refresh the air and mitigate the torrid breath of summer. The water dripping from the water pipes along the floor serve as a still efficient air-conditioning system.

Many of the plants in this section of the gardens were brought in from the New World, like for instance the great bottle-shaped "drunken tree" growing beside the goldfish pool.

Now cross through the gate into the European section. Here you will see a stylized series of ornamental flowerbeds and carefully trimmed shrubbery and trees, in the style of the best European gardeners.

Over the centuries the Kings of Spain brought to the gardens their own personal contributions. One of the corners is a Renaissance style sequence of flowerbeds, surrounding a spacious pool with in the middle a statue of Mercury by Diego de Pasquera (1576). Another corner forms the **Galería del Grutesco**, decorated with interesting frescoes.

Now follow the dividing wall toward the palace. At the end a gate opens into the Court of the Orange Trees, and crossing it you will find yourself back at the Plaza del Triunfo. A turn to the right will take you to the calle Judería, (the "Jewish Quarter" Street) a direct passageway from the Alcázar to Santa Cruz Quarter, formerly the Jewish Quarter (see "The Santa Cruz Quarter").

Other sites

We are now back in *Plaza del Triunfo*. South of the cathedral you will see the building of the **Casa Lonja** (Chamber of Commerce), seat of the *National Archives*. This large rectangular palace was built toward the end of the 16th century by Juan de Herrera, in Renaissance style. For two centuries it housed the Chamber of Commerce of Seville, until its upper floor was assigned in 1785 to the **Archivo General de Indias**, with its thousands of files, documents and deeds related to Seville's ties with the colonies.

The Archives contain also a number of collections: the annals of colonial courts of law; a collection of commercial contracts; four centuries of colonial book-keeping; and altogether, four centuries of the history of Imperial Spain. Some of the most interesting items on display are: Columbus' diaries, his correspondence, and an outstanding series of ancient maps. Historians and other researchers may peruse hundreds of manuscripts, papers, diaries and books related to the period of the great discoveries and to colonial life in the New World.

It is open to visitors Monday-Saturday, 10am-1pm. Free entrance.

Between the Alcázar and the Chamber of Commerce

there is the **Museo de Arte Contemporáneo** (1 Calle de Santo Tomás, open Tuesday-Friday 10am-7pm, Saturday and Sunday 10am-2pm).

The Santa Cruz Quarter —
the Charm of Old Alleys

A visit to the **Barrio de Santa Cruz**, the heart of Roman and Moorish Seville, is simply a must. The silence of its dark and narrow alleys (the whole quarter is closed to motorized traffic), its attractive residences, its gardens and canaries on the balconies are almost a time-traveller's experience into a forgotten past, several centuries ago.

This neighbourhood was once Seville's Jewish Quarter; its position, its elegance and its aura reflect the very special relationship that existed between the King and the Jews for many centuries, especially during the Moorish rule. The Jews were the King's respected administrative advisors and, in many other ways, his best allies. Therefore the principle was — keep them together close to the Palace. Under christian rule the Jews kept holding important positions in administration, as they did under Moslem rule, and calle Judería was serving as a direct connection between the Alcázar and their quarter. Yet, the antisemitic spirit came to Seville, as to the rest of Spain, and during 14th and 15th centuries many of them were murdered in riots and pogroms. In 1492 the Catholic Kings expel all the Jews from the kingdom, once and for all.

Today Santa Cruz is an elegant residential zone, the centre of Seville's artist and Bohèmian community. We shall lead you through its main streets to its most interesting sites; it is only a very small neighbourhood, very centrally situated, and you will have no trouble at all finding your way to it again and again.

The starting point is again the **Plaza del Triunfo**. Leave the square at its eastern corner, following the *Romero Murube* alley along the walls of the Alcázar. At number 1a you will find the interesting shop (china and local ceramics) of *La Alcazaba*; its artistic window is but a hint of the wide selection of artifacts you will find inside. Proceed along Romero Murube to *Plaza de la Alianza*. Turn right, into Rodrigo Caro, until you come to **Plaza**

SANTA CRUZ QUARTER

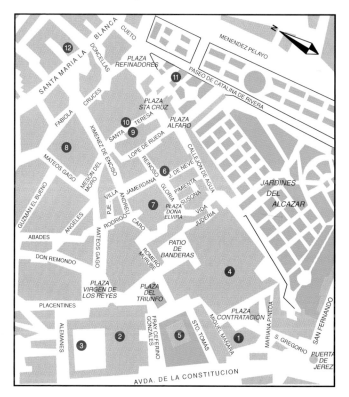

Index

Doña Elvira, a lovely square named after Elvira de Ayala, the daughter of one of the vassals of a Medieval King. Along its sides you will find several inviting open air cafés and restaurants, where you will be able to enjoy a rest in the welcome shade of some trees. In the late afternoon, street singers and musicians perform there, offering their audience the treat of their melodies (passing their hats among the crowd from time to time).

Take the next alley, left of Rodrigo Caro: Gloria St., on whose corner you will find the *Emilio Pintor Art Gallery*; most of his works portray streets and palaces of Seville, and especially his beloved Giralda. Proceed along Gloria until you come to the **Hospital de los Venerables Sacerdotes** (Hospice of the Venerable Priests). It is an impressive palace, built by architect Figueroa in the characteristic local Baroc style.

Inside the hospice you will find several paintings by Valdés Leal and sculptures by Pedro Roldán. It was built as a residence and hospice for priests and monks, and was only recently restored as a religious shelter.

Gloria St. changes into Reinoso alley, which in the past was called "Calle del Moro Muerto" — street of the Dead Moor. The legend behind that name tells the story of a Moorish gentleman, who happened to fall in love with Esther, a Jewish virgin from one of the best local families. But Esther also had a Jewish lover, a certain Barrabas, who one day met his rival in this very street and, blinded by jealousy, killed him on the spot. Neither a pleasant story, nor too original... A left turn off Reinoso will bring you to Pasaje de Villa Jamerdana, and from there a right hand turn takes you to Ximenes de Enciso, perhaps the narrowest of the many alleys in Santa Cruz.

This is where one of the several synagogues of the Judería — the Jewish Quarter as it was called in those days — once stood. When Ferdinand III conquered Seville in 1248, he received the keys of the city from a committee of Jewish elders — both as representatives of the town and as mediators between Christians and Moslems. Ferdinand's son, Alfonso the Wise, granted the Jewish community three former Mosques (that probably had once been churches...), to be transformed into synagogues. In

1492, when all Spanish Jews were forcibly exiled, the former mosque and synagogue was reinstated to what perhaps had been its first function, and became the **Church of Santa Cruz** (the Holy Cross). Then, in 1810, Napoleon's armies razed the church to the ground; all that remained was the iron cross that now stands in the middle of the square, and the name of the quarter — Santa Cruz. Seville's loving son, Murillo, is buried inside the rebuilt Chuch of Santa Cruz.

A right hand turn, at No. 8 of Santa Teresa, you will be at the **Casa de Murillo**. Bartolomé Esteban Murillo, one of Spain's greatest 17th century painters, is a true son of Seville, even more than Velázquez, who was also born in this city. Murillo's works are found in every second Sevillan church and palace, and the house where he died in 1682 has been restored as a museum of his works (open Tuesday-Sunday, 10am-2pm and 4-7pm; closed on Monday; entrance fee).

Opposite Murillo's house is the **Convento de Santa Teresa**, a 16th century Carmelitan convent. Its chapel contains several holy relics and some very beautiful 17th century carvings (open Wednesday-Sunday, 10am-2pm; closed on Mondays, Tuesdays and holidays).

From Murillo's house and the monastery, at the end of the street you will come to **Plaza de Santa Cruz**, with its large 17th century iron cross in the middle.

Behind *Plaza de Santa Cruz* is another small square, the Plaza del Alfaro, from which the famous "Barber of Seville" used to serenade his beloved Rosina.

Now turn back into the Mezquita Alley, and follow it to *Plaza de Refinadores*. The statue you see here is of Don Miguel de Maniara (more about this personage in "From the Cathedral to the River"). On the other side of the square are the **Jardines de Murillo**, perfect for a refreshing rest.

Leave *Plaza de Refinadores* through Mariscal Cruces St., and turn right into *Doncellas*. Now you come to Santa María la Blanca St. According to several sources, this is where Columbus lived at the end of the 15th century.

Judería alley

One of many plazas at the Santa Cruz Quarter

Tranquility in Santa Cruz Quarter

The **Church of Santa Maria la Blanca** is a miniature jewel of a church. Its ceilings are covered with beautifully carved wooden panels. It also has a multi-faith history: built as a mosque, in the thirteenth century it was transformed into a synagogue, and in the 16th it finally became a church. It was completely restored in 1657.

At Santa Maria la Blanca we end our first visit to Santa Cruz; but one may also turn back toward the Cathedral through Mateos Gago St., once a cobblers' street and today a string of restaurants with a nice view of the Giralda.

Another alternative is, after an invigorating coffee or lunch, to turn your attention to our next itinerary, the Quarter of St. Bartolomew (*Barrio de San Bartolomé*) just across *Calle de San José* that was once the main street of the *Judería.*

The San Bartolomé Quarter

San Bartolomé is just across the street from Santa Cruz. It is a bustling residential quarter, in which you will find several architectural and cultural gems. Unlike Santa Cruz, its houses are run-down, and the whole quarter is in urgent need of restoration. Works have already begun, in fact, but they will not be completed for at least several years.

Coming from Santa Cruz, your first stop would be the Casa de Pilatos; but our itinerary starts from the opposite end, at the Plaza Nueva bus stop.

Plaza Nueva is the main square of Seville, at the northern end of Avenida de la Constitución, with scores of buses circling at all hours around the equestrian statue of King Ferdinand III, deliverer of Seville. This is where several years ago they began to dig in earnest for the ambitious project of a Sevillan underground. The idea had to be abandoned, however, when the engineers discovered that Seville's soil would have collapsed over the first train... The building that towers over the whole square is the **Ayuntamiento** (City Hall), claimed by most Sevillans to be "the most beautiful City Hall in the whole world". Your eyes will probably confirm their claim. The *Ayuntamiento* has been the seat of local government for more than 4 centuries — and it will probably last for the next 4.

The Plaza Nueva front of City Hall has been completely refurbished — and decorated with its impressive time-piece — at the beginning of our century. Leave Plaza Nueva, following the walls of the Ayuntamiento to Plaza de San Francisco. This side of the great palace dates from the 16th century, and it is the work of Diego de Riaño. Its *Plateresco* style is revealed by its carved arches and columns, its medallions, its impressive doors and iron gates, flanked by statues of Seville's legendary fathers Heracles and Julius Caesar.

Pausing for an instant in San Francisco Square, observe

its perfection as a setting for the Holy Week main event, with thousands of people streaming to this great square from all over the city. This is where the VIPs will be seated, and this is where their forefathers used to witness the *Auto-da-Fe* executions of Inquisition times.

Turn left (eastward) to Cortina St.; the statue of Cervantes reminds you that not far from here, on Sierpes St., the great writer was imprisoned on false charges (see "The Muses of Seville"). Turn left from Cortina St. into **Plaza del Salvador**.

The **Iglesia del Salvador** (Church of the Saviour), which gave the square its name, is Seville's second most revered and most important church. It was also built upon the ruins of an ancient mosque, probably the largest shrine of those times. A new church was built in 1674 by Esteban García, but after less than one century it collapsed and had to be completely rebuilt. The large dome of the present day church is the work of Leonardo de Figueroa; admire its beautiful baroc Carrara marble floors and carved altar. The Transfiguration of Christ paintings are by Cayetano Acosta. Don't miss the **Capilla de los Desamparados** (Chapel of the destitute), with its *azulejo* decorated walls. During the Holy Week processions, some of the Church relics and statues are carried through the streets of Seville.

Leaving the church, follow Calle Alcaicería to **Plaza de Alfalfa**, where on Sunday morning you will find an open-air pet market, with scores of dogs and cats and birds on sale.

Alfalfa street goes from the square to Aguilas St. and to Plaza Pilatos.

In **Casa de Pilatos** (House of Pilate) the Plateresque style reaches its unparalleled peak. It seems incredible that within such an elaborate mantle of abstruse decoration the routine of daily life could be carried on as usual. Such an aggressive mixture of ambitious styles would seem out of place almost anywhere else, but here in Seville it seems quite natural. Open to visitors 9am-6pm (Sundays only to 2pm); entrance fee.

Casa de Pilatos used to be the residence of the Duke

SAN BARTOLOMÉ QUARTER, FROM CITY HALL TO THE FINE ARTS MUSEUM

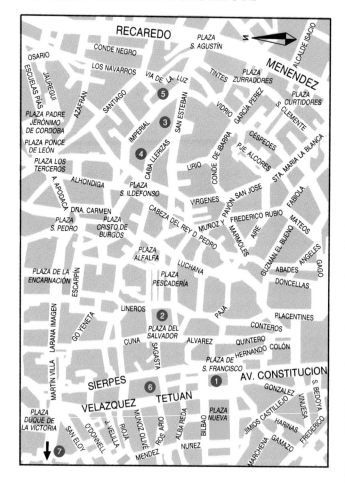

Index

1. City Hall
2. Iglesia del Salvador
3. Casa de Pilatos
4. Convento de San Leandro
5. Iglesia de San Esteban
6. Iglesia de San José
7. Fine Arts Museum

Classic architecture at Casa de Pilatos

of Medinaceli. Its original creator, Don Pedro Enriquez, Governor of Andalusia, wished to present his son, Don Federico, with a small palatial residence built in the style of the Alcázar. When Don Federico returned from a Crusade, he restored it in the style of the Holy Land. He had a host of architects, sculptors and engravers working at it for years. When the palace was finally completed, it was named House of Pilate, because according to Don Federico's memory, his palace was an exact copy of the ancient Roman Governor of Jerusalem's abode, Pontius Pilate himself.

The building is outstandingly well preserved, and is an eloquent expression of the great affluence of Sevillan gentry after the discovery of America. The richly carved marble front gate is the work of the Italian sculptor Carona. The main hall leads to a courtyard enclosed within a 24 marble arches pillared portico. Its builders used the stratagem of variously sized arches to create an illusion of wider, elongated spaces. The marble fountain set in the middle of the courtyard is the work of Aprile. Behind each of the arches stands the statue of a Roman Emperor. The courtyard itself is in *Mudéjar* style, a mixture of Moorish and Christian elements, richly decorated in stone. Among its carvings, several Arab inscriptions praise the one and only God — Allah; the owner, a staunch Catholic, evidently could not read Arabic... The *azulejo* tiles are among the most impressive in Seville, and they cover the 10 foot high walls.

The inner court opens into the Jardin Grande (Great Garden) — 11 perfectly square-shaped beds planted with palm-trees, magnolias, citruses and shrubbery. In the middle of the garden you will see a roofed fountain in Italian style, surrounded by jasmins. From inside the courtyard a royal staircase leads to the gallery and exhibition halls on the second floor, with scores of statues and paintings from the 17th and 18th century, among which you will find, in the Salón Oviedo, near the library, the *Arrastre de un Toro* by Francisco de Goya.

Having left Casa de Pilatos, stop next door, at the **Convento de San Leandro**. The original order was founded in 1295, and its nunnery was transferred here during the reign of Don Pedro I, in 1369. The present building, however, is much more recent, in the classical style of the 17th century, with several much later additions. Art lovers will enjoy Martinez Montañés' beautiful altar, in the best late-medieval style. Most visitors, however, have other, and sweeter, interests: they come to taste and buy the famous *Yemas de San Leandro*, original sweets prepared according to a very ancient recipe by the local nuns. The nunnery is open to visitors 10.30-12am. Entrance free.

Next to the nunnery is the **Iglesia de San Esteban**, in which you will recognize, like in other Sevillan former mosques, mixed elements of the *Mudéjar* and *Romanesque* styles.

Now you will be ready to return to San José St., and turning right you will be back in the centre of town. The L3 bus (Bus stop at the corner of San Esteban and Recaredo Sts.), will take you to Plaza Nueva, the starting point of this walk.

SEVILLE

The Muses of Seville —
From City Hall to the Fine Arts Museum

The starting point of this walk is on **Plaza de San Francisco**, across the square from City Hall (see "The St. Bartholomew Quarter"). From there, turn northward into **Calle Sierpes**.

Sierpes St. is one of Seville's main shopping centres. It is crowded with a kaleidoscopic of strolling, ambling and bustling multitude. As you proceed, you will remark that the side streets, which near San Francisco Square were so neat and elegant, become gradually plainer and neglected. A word of warning: Sierpes Street is not only a tourist attraction, but also a nest of molesters and pickpockets, streetwalkers and mendicants, fortune-tellers and crooks. Cervantes himself was a frequent visitor of Pierre Papin, a well known professional gambler; today gambling buffs may wish to stop at No. 28 (*Salón de Juegos Llorenas*) or at No. 35 (*Salón Café Madrid* — gambling, billiard and table-tennis). The main thing is to circulate, stopping here and there at the best shop windows, observing the crowds and absorbing its motion, without missing any of the street corners' spectacles, but keeping an eye on your wallet at all times.

Your first stop will be at No. 85. Today it is a bank, but in former centuries this building was the ill-reputed **Cárcel Real** (Royal Prison) of Seville.

The most famous inmate of that institution was most probably Miguel de Cervantes Saavedra. Born near Madrid in 1547, in his youth Cervantes joined the Spanish Army, which at that time was involved in a protracted campaign against the Ottoman Empire. He was wounded at the Battle of Lepanto (1571), and in 1575 he was taken prisoner, and held for five years by a band of Algerian

Calle Sierpes

Don Quixote — created by Cervantes inspired by Sevillan life

pirates. On his return to Spain, in spite of his poverty he took to writing in earnest. He tried to make ends meet by working as a tax collector, at best an ill-remunerated and unpopular career. More than once Cervantes, falsely accused of various crimes, ended up in some Spanish jail.

It was at Seville's Royal Prison, among its two thousand other inmates, that Cervantes began his masterpiece, *Don Quixote de la Mancha* — the story of an innocent, simple-minded dreamer, unable to come to grips with the bitter reality of his times. The book was published in 1604, 12 years before his death in 1616, and is rightly praised as one of the greatest literary works of all times. It is read, studied and admired in numerous languages to this very day.

On the wall of the building, a stone tablet commemorates the great writer — and his imprisonment here. Don Quixote, and his faithful valet Sancho Panza, have become international symbols of innocent idealism; the term "tilting at windmills", born of Don Quixote's blind fight against imaginary enemies, which he saw as threatening giants, has become proverbial in dozens of languages throughout the world.

Turn left near No. 77 into Nesta St., to visit the **Iglesia de San José**. Note the exquisite baroc chapel, rich with gold-plated wood-carvings donated to the church by its parish — the 18th century Guild of Carpenters and Woodcarvers.

At the far end of Sierpes, turn left into the bustling Martin Villa St. and to **Plaza Duque de la Victoria**, with its small jewellery and handicraft market around the statue of Velázquez. On the west side of the square you will find the large *El Corte Inglés* department store (see "Shopping in Seville"), with its attractive upper floor cafeteria.

Follow Alfonso XII St. to Plaza del Museo and to the Fine Arts Museum. It is almost a mile long walk — or a five minute ride by taxi.

The **Fine Arts Museum** (Museo de Bellas Artes) occupies the ancient Convento de la Merced, a 13th century building, of whose original *Mudéjar* style very little remains.

It was restored at the beginning of the 16th century as a Baroc palace. Destroyed by fire in 1810, after its restoration it was confiscated (together with many other possessions of the Catholic Church of Spain) and assigned to the recently founded museum. The building was restored again at the beginning of our century.

In the impressive halls of the ground floor you will find thousands of religious artifacts and implements, collected after the confiscation of scores of churches and monasteries throughout the country. The art collection of the Spanish School is undoubtedly one of the largest and most comprehensive collections of its type, what makes this museum second only to Madrid's Prado. The upper floor art collections, covering a span of less than seven centuries, from the 13th to the 19th, include tiles, ceramics, paintings and sculptures. The upper floor was designed by Figueroa, one of the greatest local architects of all times. The paintings are presented in chronological order, and you can easily follow the development stages of the Spanish School. In 15th century works, the Gothic style is predominant. Then you will recognize, specially in Bermejo's *San Juan Batista*, the influence of the Dutch-Spanish School. El Greco (portrait of his son Manuel), Velázquez (portrait of Suarez de Ribera), and Goya (portrait of Don José Duaso), are all duly represented in the main gallery.

The Fine Arts Museum will give you a clear view of Spanish painting, from the great works of El Greco, Velázquez, Zurbarán, Valdés Leál, Ribera, Murillo, Goya and others to several less known 19th century artists. An entire hall is dedicated to Murillo. Here you can get a good idea of the school of art, which emphasizes the freshness of picture and paint.

It is here that many visitors will make their first contact with Francisco Pacheco (1564-1644), father of a local school of painting, whose pupils often competed successfully with the best contemporary Venetian and Florentine artists. The work of all these painters is also exhibited in several churches and museums in Seville and elsewhere, but you will only find them together at the Fine Arts Museum as parts of a harmonious and comprehensive whole.

A street corner in the centre of town

The Museum is open Tuesday-Sunday, 9.30am-2.30pm; entrance fee.

La Caridad Church

SEVILLE

From the Cathedral to the River

At 24 Avenida de la Constitución, across the street from the closed western doors of the Great Cathedral, you will see a copper archway, the starting point of our next itinerary. The archway leads to the elegant, semi-circular **Plaza del Cabildo** — the Mecca of local stamp and coin collectors. This plaza is in fact an enclosed courtyard, on whose grounds resides the *Mercadillo Filatélico* (active Sundays from mid-morning to early afternoon). Here one can find not only Spanish stamps and coins, but also a number of ancient coins, often found in the fields by farmers. Before buying old coins, however, be warned that their export requires filing for (and obtaining) a specific permit. Moreover, beware of copies and counterfeits!

Now turn into Almirantazgo St.; then turn right, passing through the wide **Pasaje Seises** gate, built in 1573 as an addition to the adjacent monastery. Today the gate opens into Dos de Mayo St. Behind the left-side wall is the Maestranza de Artillería (the Artillery Barracks). This was the Headquarters of Falangist General Queipo de Llano at the beginning of the Spanish Civil War. In July 1936 he took over the city in Franco's name and destroyed the stronghold of the Republicans, the Triana Quarter, with gunfire. Turn left into Temprado St., and follow it to the **Hospital de la Caridad**.

This hospital resides in one of Seville's most elegant palaces, built by Miguel de Mañara, a highborn exponent of the 17th century aristocracy of Seville, who having repented his sins, joined the *Hermandad de la Caridad* (a local religious order) and spent his last years (from 1662 to 1679) as a simple orderly in his new hospital. Posterity, however, tends to remember him less for his later good deeds, than for his earlier exploits, which made of him one of the archetypal models of Don Juan.

The "Order of the Charity" was founded in the middle of the 16th century by Pedro Martínez, to provide burial rites for the condemned, the pauper and those drowned in the river. This was performed in the *Capilla de los Ahorcados* (the Chapel of the hanged). The new order expanded slowly to cater not only for the dead, but also for the dying, and thus the need arose for a new hospice for the terminally ill.

Miguel de Mañara was born in 1627 to a rich and noble Sevillan family. After several years as an incorrigible playboy, at the age of 35, having passed out in a streetfight, he had a vision of his own death and burial. Deeply shocked by this experience, he decided to join the Order of Charity, opening a new leaf and becoming one of that order's most devoted volunteers. One year later he was elected head of the order, and undertook the building of its new hospice. The life of Miguel de Mañara was the subject of a biography by Juan de Cárdenas; later that book inspired the French playwriter Blaze de Bury, who incorporated Miguel's rowdiest exploits in his personage — Don Juan (see "Culture and Arts" in the introduction).

Above the hospital door you will see the stone inscription *Domus Pauperorum Scala Coeli* (Heaven's Ladder Poorhouse). Inside a small garden, on its right side, is the hospital entrance. The hospital chapel has a beautiful altar (1674, built by Pineda and decorated by Roldán); its walls depict several great works of art, among which 7 (once 12, but 5 are now dispersed in several art museums), originally painted by Murillo on Miguel de Mañara's appointment. Above the chapel doors you will see the *Jeroglíficos de la Muerte* paintings by Valdés Leál. These striking works show the dead bodies disfigured and worm-eaten, under the legend *Finis Gloriœ Mundi* (End of the World Glory), and a second background inscription *Ni más ni Menos* (Neither more, nor less). In this chapel, together with other members of his order, lie the remains of Miguel de Mañara. The site is open to visitors (entrance fee), Monday-Friday 10am-1pm and 3.30-6pm, and Sundays 10.30-12.30am.

Proceed now toward the river, beyond the *Teatro de la Maestranza*. Cross the Paseo de Cristóbal Colón, approaching the **Torre del Oro** (Golden Tower).

This once magnificent dodecagonal tower is but a shadow of its past pomp. Even the yellowish tiles on its wall have

SEVILLE

FROM THE CATHEDRAL TO THE RIVER, THE WORLD BEYOND THE RIVE ―

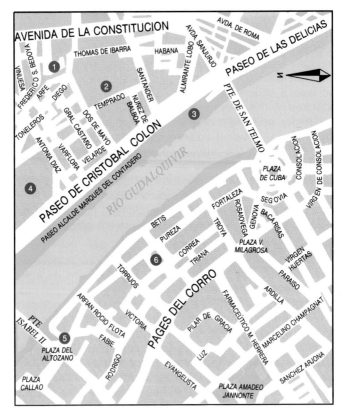

Index

lost most of the glimmer that gave the tower its illusory name. Built in the first half of the 12th century, the Golden Tower was, in the Almohads period, a component of the defensive structure of the Alcázar, connected by a thick

The Torre del Oro

iron chain, with a twin structure, called the "Silver Tower", on the opposite bank of the river. The two towers and their chain were intended to prevent, or at least delay, an eventual naval invasion. But in 1248, when Ramón de Bonifaz, one of King Ferdinand III's generals, breached the chain, the town fell. The "Silver Tower" disappeared, and the surviving bastion became first a jail, then a gold and silver storing facility and a symbol of home to faraway sailors. Today it houses a modest **Naval Museum**, with an interesting collection of old maps and instruments portraying Seville's ties with the Ocean and with the New World. Open Tuesday-Friday, 10am-2pm, Saturday and Sunday 10am-1pm. Entrance fee.

After visiting the Golden Tower, you may stroll along the Alfonso XIII Canal on the Paseo Alcalde Marqués Contadero. This is not the Guadalquivir river, but a watercourse, that branches off the river and returns to it, creating the island of La Cartuja. Most river cruises follow the canal southward, rounding back to the river. All Seville's greatest palaces and monuments may be viewed from the canal and from the river from a new and catching perspective. In summer the cruises start at 1.15pm, 4pm, 5.45pm and 7.30pm, with a night cruise at 10.15pm. One may also hire a rowboat, across the river from the Golden Tower.

Further north, beyond several restaurants and observation sites, you will come to the **Plaza de Toros de la Maestranza**.

The bullfight arenas of Spain are the object of all Spaniards' pride. To be considered a "great city", a Spanish town must be able to show off a great **Plaza de Toros**. The citizens of Merida, or Cartagena, are proud to tell the story of their arenas, built on the foundations of ancient Mitran temples. Seville has good reason to be proud of its Maestranza — one of the most praised and grandest Plazas de Toro in Spain.

The Maestranza Arena was built in 1760-63 in classic style and in the traditional colours of Seville: golden, white and red. All the most famous *matadores* have performed here: Juan Belmonte, Joselito, Romero, Chicuelo and others built their great fame within these walls. Their exploits have been repeatedly illustrated by many great artists and writers, such as Goya, Picasso and Hemingway.

The site is open to visitors (except on *Corrida* days), 10am-1.30pm; entrance fee — only a fraction of the entrance ticket to the *corridas*...

Now to a welcome refreshment and rest at one of the restaurants that line the square, especially between Adriano and Antonia Diaz streets, on whose walls you will find posters and illustrations of past bull-fighting glories.

The World Beyond the River —
Triana and Los Remedios

EXPO '92 lures large crowds across the Alfonso XIII Canal — but only a few bother to spend some of their time strolling through the quarters of *Triana* and *Los Remedios*. **Triana**, a neighbourhood named after the Roman Emperor Trajan (a son of neighbouring Italica), will offer you the opportunity to spend a very pleasant, although "different" afternoon.

Those who wish to absorb some of this popular quarter's unique atmosphere should cross the river on Puente Isabel II. On **Plaza del Altozano**, on the other side of the river, you will see the statue of one of the greatest local *Matadores*, Juan Belmonte, *El Pasmo de Triana* (The Wonder of Triana). At the southern end of the square you will find the **Mercado** (Covered Market) **of Triana**. It is mainly a fish and seafood market: the people of Triana were seamen and fishermen for many centuries. Near the market is the **Callejón de la Inquisición** (Alley of the Inquisition), so named because of its proximity to the Inquisition Headquarters.

Having visited the market, follow the river southward on **Calle Betis**. Enjoy the skylight across the river. Turn right from Calle Betis into Duarte, to the **Iglesia de Santa Ana**, the main church of *Triana* and starting point of many a Holy Week procession. It is a very old church, built by King Alfonso X in the 13th century. You will recognize in its structure four different styles: Moorish, Romanesque, Gothic and, in the belltower, Mudéjar. The *retablo* (altar wall) is in Plataresque style, and is one of the most remarkable in town.

Tired? Hot? Weary of so many churches? Turn right, and on the way to the San Telmo Bridge make your own choice among several pleasant river-front cafés. After a well-earned rest, turn right at the bridge and you will find yourself on **Plaza de Cuba**, at the far end of

The Guadalquivir

Betis Street

the elegant Avenida de la Republica Argentina, easily recognzied by its palmtree avenues.

Across the Avenida is the **Los Remedios** Quarter, that in recent years has become a Sevillan shoppers' paradise. Avenida Republica Argentina and Avenida Asunción vaunt some of the best and most elegant shops in town, together with numerous bank branches and other businesses. The Avenida Republica Argentina ends at Plaza de la República Dominicana. With all those Latin-American names, one will not be allowed to forget Seville's special historic ties with the New World...

From the Centre to the Maria Luisa Park

This walk will take you from the bustling heart of modern Seville to the relaxing atmosphere of this city's major park — the **Maria Luisa Park**.

Start at the southern end of Avenida da la Constitución, near the **Puerta de Jerez** (Jerez Gate) and its fountain. This is where the southern gate of the city walls once stood. It is named after the town of *Jerez de la Frontera* (see "Excursions"); today all that remains is the name: the walls and the gate have disappeared. The small chapel you see on the northern side of the square, in the *Mudéjar* style, is the last remains of the first University of Seville. In 1936 the **Yanduri Palace** was the firefront of Franco Falangistas in the Spanish Civil War. This is in fact Franco's first command post, on his arrival from Morocco at the very beinnings of the war. The future dictator of Spain had been invited by the aristocratic owners of the palace. The palace is also the birthplace of Vicente Aleixandre, (1977 Nobel Price for Literature).

The garden you see along Avenida Roma, south of Puerta de Jerez, is the **Jardin de Cristina**. Across the garden is the **Palacio de San Telmo**, with its impressive baroc front, decorated with statues, carved columns and floral motives in marble. The palace was built in the 18th century by architect Figueroa, to house the *Universidad de Mareantes* (University of Seamanship), named after St. Telmo, the patron Saint of all seafarers. The statues that decorate its front are a real gallery of Seville's greatest artists: Murillo, Velázquez and others. Today it houses a teachers' college and is closed to visitors.

At the corner of Avenida Roma and Avenida San Fernando stands the **Hotel King Alfonso XIII**, pride of Sevillan hotels and a first rank monument on its own. This hotel, designed to look like a medieval castle, was inaugurated in 1928, toward the International Exhibition of 1929, and its guest-book has often been signed by scores of kings, princes,

FROM THE CENTRE
TO THE MARIA LUISA PARK

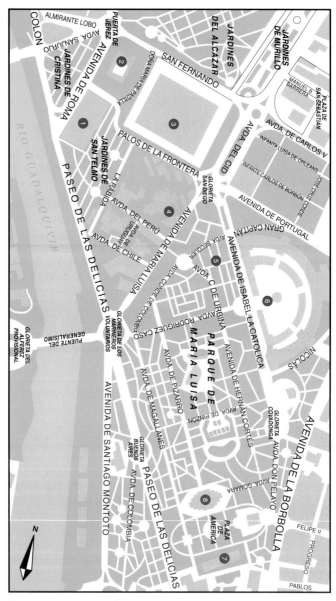

The University of Seville

Lope de Vega Theatre

presidents and heads of governments. Its patio, galleries and lobby are the showcase of its treasures: artifacts, coloured tiles, period furniture, tapestries and carpets complete the picture of what Sevillans rightly call "The Pride of Andalusia".

Proceed along San Fernando Ave., to the wide entrance gate of the **University of Seville**. This enormous building was originally built by the great architect Sebastian van der Borcht, to house the *Antigua Fabrica de Tabacos*, an 18th century tobacco factory.

Inside the main lobby you will see a magnificent stained glass ceiling. In its old industrial days, this building provided the background to Prosper Mérimée's Carmen tragedy. Mérimée's work was later used by Bizet in his famous opera.

The tobacco industry of Seville was more than a century old in the 18th century; in fact, it had grown so rapidly from its early 17th century beginnings, that the construction of a suitable site had become an urgent necessity. By the middle of the 19th century, however, it had become too large, too cumbersome and too costly — and the *Antigua Fabrica de Tabacos* was only too happy to sell it — and to see it transformed into the Faculty of Sciences of the Seville University, an ancient and respected institution founded by the Catholic Kings and the Pope. The Jesuite Order had taken over the management of the university after two centuries of slow academic decline, and in a short while they were able to attract some of the best teachers in Europe to their school. Hundreds of students flocked to Seville to learn under the new teachers, until in 1850 the palace was purchased and adapted to the requirements of the university. The building is open to visitors Monday-Friday, 8am-9pm, Saturdays 9am-1pm. Entrance free.

Now turn right into the Avenida del Cid. At the corner of Calle Palos de la Frontera and Avenida de María Luisa you will see the beautiful **Teatro Lope de Vega**. All the splendours of Sevillan architecture are here reflected. The rounded front of the palace is richly decorated with sculptures and stuccos in the characteristic Sevillan white and ochre shades.

Across the avenue, in front of the theatre, are the gates to the **Maria Luisa Park** (Parque de María Luisa) — and several attractive open-air cafés, perfect for a short relaxing pause during your walk. The grounds are the gift (1893) of Princess María Luisa Fernanda de Borbón to the City of Seville.

In 1910 the city founders comissioned Jean Claude le Forestier (a famous French garden architect) to design a park site "worthy of the Alcázar Gardens" for these grounds. Following this mandate and his imagination, le Forestier created a park site "blessed with many waters, whose gurgle will be heard by its visitors even from its farthest corners". The park itself is subdivided into several large square sections, rich with streamlets and water-jets, each with its own central square *glorieta* — a central monument dedicated to various local themes.

Proceed now along Avenida de Isabel la Católica, the gardens' main throughfare; near the entrance you will see the modest but charming and intimate *glorieta* dedicated to Gustavo Adolfo Bécquer, Seville's 17th century romantic poet. The **Plaza de España** castle, on the other side of the avenue, is characteristic of the most bombastic aspects of Seville: turrets and pinnacles, bulwarks and drawbridges, stiff gardens and artificial lakes — all that may catch the eye is present here.

This castle, as many other structures here, was erected on the occasion of the *Exposición Ibero-Americana* of 1929. The castle housed the Spanish pavillion of that great International Exhibition. On its ground floor each Spanish region was allotted its own hall, decorated with its own characteristic objects and motifs, maps and *azulejos*. In the main gallery you will see a sequence of city maps in alphabetic order. The best spots reserved are naturally, for Seville itself... Whatever your personal taste, a visit to this palace is a must. Today the palace is the seat of the regional administration of Andalusia — and the local Military Command.

After Plaza de España, you may go on to explore the gardens — by foot or by coach. At the end of your stroll you should reach the opposite side of the gardens at the Plaza de América. This is the site of the American Pavillion at the

A glorieta in Maria Luiza Park

1929 Exhibition. Today it houses the **Museo Arquelógico**, with its vaste collections of artifacts of the Stone and Bronze Ages. Most visitors, however, come to see The *Carambolo Treasures*, in halls 5 and 6. Tartessian solid gold artifacts from the 5th century BC were found in 1958 at the Carambolo site, less than 3 miles from Seville. The main floor is dedicated to Roman Seville: statues and shards, mosaics and capitals brought here from the Italica site (see "Excursions"). Particularly striking is the 2nd century BC statue of Hermes, undoubtedly one of Spain's best examples of Roman classical sculpture. The museum is open Tuesday-Sunday, 10am-2pm; closed on Mondays and holidays. Entrance fee.

The adjoining **Museo de Arte y Costumbres Populares** (Museum of Popular Art and Folklore) tries to reconstruct images of daily Spanish life throughout the centuries. There are sets of rural rooms, farming tools, hand-looms, potters-wheels, vine-presses, silversmiths' tools etc. In another section you will find the world of the haves: coaches, costumes, snuff-boxes and jewels.

Back from the two museums, you may wander along

Plaza de España

Le Forestier's paths, stopping from time to time at an attractive fountain or artificial lake, or before some of the most impressive *glorietas*, with their enticing wooden seats.

You may also leave the square toward Las Delicias St., turning left to follow the edge of the gardens. Across the street you will see several 1929 structures, built in a variety of styles. Today they house libraries, educational institutions and public offices. On the **Glorieta Buenos Aires** you will see the national hero of Argentina, General San Martin, who won that country its independence from Spain — his presence here is a striking example of Spanish liberalism and open mindedness. You will end this walk at the corner of Avenida Maria Luisa, where you will find a branch of the Tourist Information Office in what was the miniature pavillion of Guatemala at the exhibition.

It is not advisable to frequent the gardens after dark (there is a Police Station inside the Park).

The Northern Quarters

Unlike the centre, with its many historic sites and its hectic bustle, the northern quarters present an image of stark poverty and neglect. Nevertheless, here too you will come across some interesting sites and architectural gems.

Leave Plaza de la Concordia walking northward on Gran Poder St., and turn left into Conde de Barajas, until you reach Plaza de San Lorenzo, not far from the *El Corte Inglés* department store. This is, with the **Iglesia de San Lorenzo**, one of Seville's major religious centres. The Capilla de Nuestro Padre Jesús del Gran Poder is a splendid example of religious architecture and art.

The St. Lorenzo Church was built upon the foundations of a 13th century *Mudéjar* church, and some of its relics and art treasures go back these times. Don't miss the 17th century painting of **La Virgen de Rocamodor**, within its beautiful, and much older Gothic panel.

The impressive Gothic Crucifix by Juan de Mesa (1620), behind the Chapel's altar, represents Nuestro Padre Jesús del Gran Poder. On Good Friday, during the Holy Week festival, thousands flock from all parts of the city to worship Jesus of the Great Power. On other days the church and chapel are open to visitors, free, 8am-1.30pm and 6-9pm.

Next, proceed along Calle Santa Clara. The next interesting site is the **Convento de Santa Clara**, a 15th century palace. Its lines and motifs are characteristic of the transition period between the Romanesque and the Gothic styles. Both styles are clearly reflected in the two levels of the 13th century **Torre de Don Fadrique**, adjacent to the monastery. While its first floor is a classic example of Romanesque architecture, the upper level is distinctly Gothic.

Don Fadrique fought for the *Reconquista* of Seville in 1248. Then, having been granted lands of his own in Germany, he left for his fief, only to return to Seville in 1271. Shortly

THE NORTHERN QUARTERS

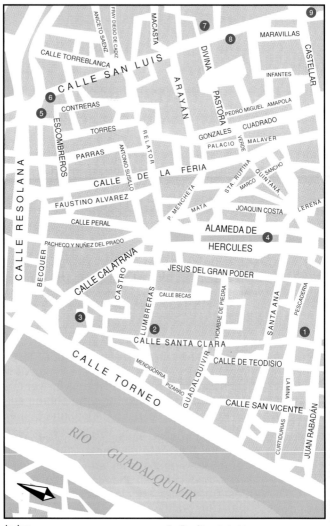

thereafter, however, he became involved in a conspiracy against his brother, King Alfonso X, and was imprisoned here, and this is how the tower got its name. From the top of the tower you will be able to enjoy a wide open view of the city and the river; inside the tower there is a modest archaeological museum.

The Monastery is open to visitors daily 10.30-12am; the Tower only Monday-Thursday, 11am-2pm. Free entrance to the monastery — but tickets must be bought to visit the tower and its museum.

Not far north of Santa Clara, on the bank of the Guadalquivir, you will see the oldest Monastery in Seville, the **Convento de San Clemente**. It was built soon after the *Reconquista*, in the second half of the 13th century. The convent church is interesting not only for its characteristic *Mudéjar* style, but also for its exceptional ceilings, its gold decorations by Montañés and the large paintings by Francisco Pacheco and by Valdez Léal. The bridge that crosses the Guadalquivir near the monastery is the **Puente de la Barqueta** (Bridge of the little Boat), built only recently for EXPO '92.

Calatrava St. will now take you eastward to **Alameda de Hércules**. Little remains of the past glories of this once imposing avenue, named after one of the legendary fathers of the city. It has been so severely neglected, that the only sign of its past splendour is the statuary standing on the columns, high above the crowds. On Sunday mornings the avenue becomes a vast flea market — and this is when it is really worth a visit.

La Macarena

East of the Alameda de Hércules you will see the **La Macarena** quarter, a noisy and crowded residential district with several interesting churches.

The most important is undoubtedly **Basílica de la Macarena**, whose full name is "*La Virgen Maria Santísima de la Esperanza Macarena*". The Lady in question is, it goes without saying, the Virgin Mary, as reproduced in black by an unknown sculptor. This statue, with its expressive face, its rich clothes, its jewels and its diamond tears, has become one of the most popular centres of worship, not only in Seville, but in all Andalusia. Religious feelings reach their peak during the Holy Week, and in particular on Good Thursday and Friday.

You will find the statue within the Basílica de la Macarena, a modern church built in the 40s of our century by Gomez Millán. Near the basílica stands the **Iglesia de San Gil**, where the statue of the Macarena used to stand. San Gil was severely damaged in 1936, during the Spanish Civil War, and the Statue was taken in custody by one of its faithful believers, who returned it safely, after the war.

The Basílica is open to visitors daily, 9am-1pm and 5-9pm. The Church vaults open 30 minutes after opening hours, and close 30 minutes before closing hours. Entrance fee.

The arch of the **Puerta de la Macarena** is, together with the remains of the old Roman **Muralla** (Wall), one of the rare remnants of the old city walls. The gate is, however, almost a reconstruction, restored in Baroc style.

If you have not had your fill of churches, turn southward, back toward the centre, on Calle San Luiz. Several side streets lead to a series of churches. The first on your left is the **Iglesia de Santa Marina**. Its belltower used to be a Mosque's minaret eight centuries ago. Across the street you will see the **Iglesia de San Luiz**. Further south you will come to a beautiful old minaret, now the belltower of the **Iglesia de San Marcos**.

Musts

The Capital of Andalusia is full of first class art treasures and historic sites. Its churches, palaces and other monuments, its parks and gardens will always be remembered. Here is a short list of the sites that, however short your visit, are really a must.

The Cathedral: One of the largest churches, and the largest Gothic church in the world. Great paintings, sculptures and bas-reliefs, tombs of kings and of Columbus. See "The Cathedral and the Alcázar".

La Giralda: The ancient minaret that became the cathedral's belltower — and the symbol of Seville (not less than Big Ben for London or the Statue of Liberty for New York). See "The Cathedral and the Alcázar".

The Alcázar: The ruler's seat of power for many centuries; a sequence of different styles and atmospheres; royal apartments, gardens, courtyards and galleries. See "The Cathedral and the Alcázar".

Archivo de Indias: An Archive and Museum of the Age of Discovery, in the halls of an impressive old palace. Ancient maps, thousands of manuscripts — and Columbus' diaries and correspondence. See "The Cathedral and the Alcazar".

Santa Cruz Quarter: The former Jewish Quarter, now an inviting quarter, a labyrinth of alleys and courtyards and old churches within former synagogues. See "The Santa Cruz Quarter".

Casa de Pilatos: An old aristocratic mansion, that would not fit anywhere else in the world. See "The St. Bartolomew Quarter".

Fine Arts Museum: Spain's second most important art museum (after Madrid's Prado), set in a former monastery. Religious art — and a panoramic vista of the great Spanish School of Painting throughout the centuries.

The Giralda towers above Santa Cruz

Hospital de la Caridad: Miguel de Mañara's penance token to the poor and the ill of Seville; in its chapel, some of the most striking paintings of Valdés Leál. See "Between the Cathedral and the river".

Maria Luisa Park: Seville's beautiful main park, with the **Plaza de España** built for the 1929 International Exhibition. See "From the Centre to the Maria Luisa Park".

La Cartuja: The island enclosed by the Guadalquivir and the Alfonso XIII Canal, with EXPO '92 and the beautiful Las Cuevas Monastery. See "EXPO '92".

Excursions

Itálica

Only 4 miles past Seville is the ancient site of Itálica, the Roman provincial capital, founded in the 3rd century BC. It served as a garrison town in the course of the long struggle for supremacy between Rome and Carthago. Its large amphitheatre and its outstanding mosaic floors indicate that Italica was at some time one of Rome's richest provincial centres — much more than a military outpost.

How to get there

Driving your own car, follow the Italica Road to the village of Camas, 3 miles from town. This village, which today is a residential suburb of Seville, lies at the foot of the **Carambolo** hill, where many *Tartassian* gold artifacts and jewels from the Archaeological Museum were originally found (see "From the Centre to the *Maria Luisa Park*"). Not far from **Camas** are the cellars of *Vino de Pasas*, (a raisin wine famous throughout Spain and abroad). There is not much to see at the Carambolo digs, and we suggest you omit them from your itinerary.

One mile past Camas you will find yourself in **Santiponce**. Many of its houses stand on ancient Roman foundations. The site has not yet been fully researched, and ancient shards are often revealed in the course of local building works. A comprehensive excavation of the site has been repeatedly delayed, probably since it may destroy many modern dwellings in the area.

Itálica was founded in 205 BC by *Scipio*, who had crossed from Africa to Spain in pursuit of the defeated Carthaginian Armies. The Roman general fell in love with the region, and selected this site for his new garrison town. The town occupied an area of about 130 acres and included residences, a theatre, an amphitheatre, baths and several sanctuaries. In its heyday, it had a population of more than

10,000 people, and was used as a resort and recreation centre for the provincial legions. The most famous sons of Itálica are without doubt its two Roman Emperors: Trajan, and Adrian, who did their best to expand and develop the town.

The Roman ruins are very impressive. The spacious amphitheatre (120 by 500 feet!) had seating capacity for more than 25,000 people. Clearly, it was intended not only for the permanent inhabitants of Itálica, but rather as a main facility for the whole province and its garrison. In later times the amphitheatre was repeatedly raided and looted; its pillars and stones were used in newer buildings and river embankments; its ornaments and capitals were incorporated in villas and temples until only its skeleton remained. The theatre was erected in the first century AD, and later restored by Adrian. Although only fragments have survived centuries of plunder, the villas' mosaic floors are still spectacular, in the best style of Imperial Rome.

Having visited the site, a stop at the local museum will complete the picture: it contains hundreds of tablets, inscriptions, fragments, capitals, columns and statues. Entrance fee.

The Santiponce **Monasterio de San Isidoro del Campo** is also worth a stop: built in the 14th century, it has one of the most beautiful Montañés *retablo* (altar wall), a striking *Mudéjar* cloister and the 14th century tomb of its founder, Alonso Pérez de Guzman.

Toward Cordoba

Carmona

Carmona is a charming little old town, 20 miles from Seville on the *Cordoba* road. It may be reached by bus (the Seville-Ecija-Cordoba line has a stop there) — or by car. Its first settlement dates from the Neolithic Period. It was one of the main centres of the *Tartessian* culture and it owed its affluence to its rich agricultural soil. The Romans made it into one of their principal trade centres. During the later centuries of the Moorish rule, Carmona was for a time an independent *taifa*. Carmona was "reconquered" by the Christian armies in 1247 and has continued ever since to prosper as a market town and religious centre, with a population of 25,000 people.

Carmona

What to see

The two major Roman remains are the *Necropolis* "City of the Dead" and the Amphitheatre. In the **Necropolis** you will find several interesting tombs; one of the most monumental is called **Tumba del Elefante**. It is a spacious mausoleum, fully equipped with sitting room, dining room and... kitchen, with the statue of an elephant at the

AROUND SEVILLE

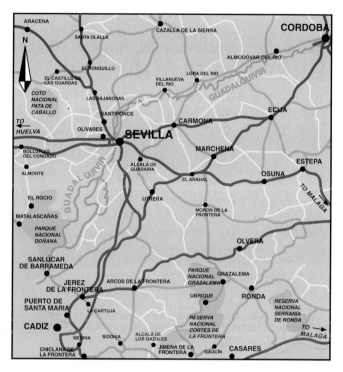

place of honour. According to some archaeologists, this was the site of an unknown cult. Perhaps the elephant commemorates Hannibal's passage, Carthago's avenger on his way to Rome... The Elephant's Tomb was the first to be discovered, more than 130 years ago; since then, hundreds of tombs and mausoleums have been excavated. Several of the most interesting fragments are exhibited at the adjoining **museum**. Necropolis and museum are open to visitors Tuesday-Sunday, 10am-2pm. Entrance fee.

Another interesting ruin is that of the **Puerta de Seville**, a Roman archway, to which the Moors added a small rampart, the **Alcázar de la Puerta de Seville**. A second, higher rampart, the **Alcázar del Rey don Pedro Arriba**, belongs to the Moorish period. Both were restored and buttressed after the *Reconquista*, to provide the town with at least some defense and to serve as a princely residence. Today part of the complex is preserved as a historic site, while another part has been restored as a hotel.

The church of *Santa María*, one of several local Gothic churches, was built on the ruins of an old mosque, whose components can be still recognized in the mixed style structure of the church.

Ecija

On your way to Cordoba, Ecija provides you with a pleasant stop, 50 miles out of Seville. It is yet another town founded more than 25 centuries ago. At first it went under the Greek name of *Astigi*. The Roman newcomers built it into a regional stronghold named *Colonia Augusta Firma Astigi*.

Ecija is one of the hottests spots in Spain, with summer maximum temperatures frequently topping 100F and peaks of over 115F. It is an olive oil production centre, and its heat and oil have joined in getting it nicknamed "The Frying Pot of Andalusia".

Ecija stands on a hillside, surrounded by several large farms, its main branch is bull-raising for Spain's corridas. It is a town of farmers and traders, with a population of more than 35,000 people.

Step off the car (or bus) at **Plaza de España**, near the **Church of Santa María**, built in the 18th century on the site of an old mosque. In the church courtyard is a small archaeological museum, with a selection of fragments from the Roman period and from later times. In the **Church of Santa Cruz** you will find several early-Christian *sarcófagos*. The **Peñaflor Palace** has an unusual *Renaissance* style front, with carved stone decorations and large frescoes.

There are several interesting churches and 11 belltowers — all of them replicas of famous towers in various Spanish cities. The Sanza Cruz belltower is the tallest and most striking of all.

After this short visit, it is time to return to your car, or to the bus, and to carry on to Cordoba.

Cordoba

Cordoba is on the banks of the Guadalquivir, some 80 miles east of Seville. It is about 380 feet above sea level, and connected to Seville by an excellent throughway; by car, it is less than 90 minutes away.

Cordoba was already a town of some importance as far back as the year 152 BC, when the Romans made it their regional centre. During the Visigoth period, it was the seat of an important bishopric. Later, under the Moors, Cordoba was for a time the Capital of Moorish Spain and the seat of its Caliphs. Soon after his conquest of the town in 756, Caliph Abed-el-Rahman I undertook the construction of the Great Mosque (see below) and of his own residence. In the 11th century, however, under the new dynasty, Cordoba lost much of its former importance. In 1236 it was taken by King Ferdinand III, "the Saint", of Castilla y Léon, conqueror of Seville.

For a time the Catholic kings maintained their residence in Cordoba, but it never recovered the status it had enjoyed under the Moors. In 1927 it was proclaimed the capital of its region, and the administration offices contribute considerably to its prosperity and growth. Today 250,000 people leave in the city.

Cordoba is famous for its silver jewelry, so eminently visible at every other shop window.

The throughway from Seville crosses Cordoba's industrial zone and comes to the Guadalquivir. Turn right onto Avenida de la Confederación, the riverside avenue that ends at the Roman bridge. Stop for a quick panoramic view across the river, facing the city. You will see two remarkable large buildings: on your left the **Cordoba Alcázar**, on the right the **Great Mosque** — our next stop.

Before the **Roman Bridge** stands its ancient guardhouse. Cross the bridge, and on the other side you will come to the gate of the Roman city, whose foundations are almost hidden six feet below the street.

Walk around the gate and turn left into Avenida del Alcázar. Proceed along the riverside and turn right on Avenida Corregidor, the city's main street. Walking

CORDOBA — THE OLD CITY

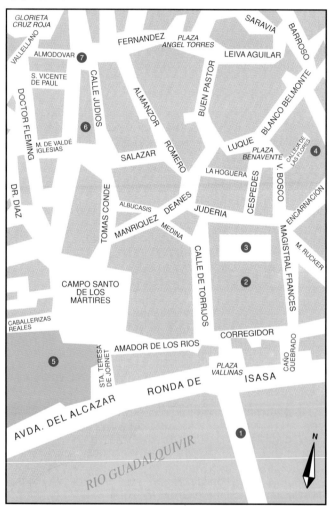

Index
1. Roman Bridge
2. Mezquita
3. Alcázar
4. Patio de los Naranjos
5. Synagogue
6. Almodóvars gate

Cordoba — the Roman bridge

through the streets of Cordoba you will find proof of the unique relationship of Andalusia with the three great monotheistic religions: the predominant influence of the Catholic Church, the Islamic undertones of its past and the subtle influence of several centuries of rich Jewish spiritual life.

The Islamic component is most evident at the **Mezquita**, the great mosque-cathedral of Cordoba. All the Catholics, who come week after week to Mass in this cathedral, have only one name for it — the Mezquita, the Mosque... The Mezquita is open to visitors 10.30am-1.30pm; summer afternoons 4-7pm and winter afternoons 3.30-5.30pm.

When Abed-el-Rahman set himself up in Cordoba, in the second half of the 8th century, he determined that this town would become "the Mecca of the West". Accordingly, he selected his best architects and builders for the construction of one of the greatest mosques in the world. When it was completed, in all its four stages, the mosque had a total of 1113 columns! Even now, when so many have been eliminated or incorporated within its walls, 856 can still be counted.

Abed-el-Rahman's architects had columns of every size and shape brought in even from distant sites. The great variety of these ancient columns and capitals gives the Mezquita a quaint character, at first sight, as if it were an archaeological museum of sorts. Only in the last stage, when the supply of old columns had been exhausted, did the builders begin to make their own according to their architects' specifications. The problems caused by the need to obtain a single level, while using columns of different sizes was solved, as you will see, using bases and capitals of different dimensions.

Enter through the **Puerta de los Deanes**. You will find yourself at the entrance to the most ancient stage, the **Patio de los Naranjos** (The Courtyard of the Orange Trees), with its small pools and water-jets (used in Moslem times for the ceremonial cleansing of the feet). You will see the 10th century minaret on your left; after the *Reconquista* it became the cathedral's belltower. On your right you will see a long archway, that was permanently walled up several centuries later. Cross the courtyard to the inner entrance, and turn right. Proceed to the seventh row of columns, and you will find yourself inside the oldest part of the Mezquita. Observe the double archway, and the sense of great height. The original ceiling was in carved wood, and has long since disappeared, except for some small restored fragments.

Turn left toward the structure enclosing the Mezquita great inner spaces of the Cathedral. But before you enter, observe the complex's second stage, Abed-el-Rahman II's contribution, with its nine rows of columns.

Further on there is a wide space, unobstructed with columns. It is the third stage, built in 961 by Alhaken II. This was to become the first cathedral, as conceived by King Ferdinand III in the second half of the 13th century. Eight rows of columns were eliminated, while the rest were buttressed and strengthened in order to provide sufficient support to the structure, with its upper windows and new, higher ceilings.

Beyond the third stage is the Mihrab, the Moslem prayer niche. Its mosaics were Byzantine emperor Constantine VII's present to Cordoba; the ravages of time have been only recently restored. Stand before the Mihrab and raise your head to admire the magnificent dome. Observe the expansion of the ornamental motifs stemming from the capitals upward. This is one of the most splendid examples of Moorish architecture still standing.

The Mihrab niche, shaped like a seashell, has the acustic qualities necessary to transmit the officiant's voice to all four corners of the enormous vault.

Now turn left. On your right you will have the **Capilla del Cardenal**, on your left the **Capilla Real**. Proceed beyond three more rows of columns. This is the fourth stage of the complex, built in 937 by Almanzor.

Almanzor gave the Mezquita a new direction off its original southward focus, and doubled the total area of the structure. Unlike his predecessors, who were able to use an existing supply of columns, he was forced to build all components from scratch. Therefore, his columns and capitals are all made of the same grey stone, of a single size, and the motifs of their capitals are in the same style.

Now you will get into the cathedral itself, deep within the heart of the Mezquita. It was built in the 16th century, during the reign of Carlos V. The King wished to preserve the already ancient, venerable structure; but Bishop Alonso Manrique could not be stopped, and in 1523 construction began, in spite of the King's and the people's reluctance.

Carlos did not hesitate to punish both the bishop and his architect Hernán Ruiz I by death. But the damage had already been done and construction went on for two generations, under the architects Hernán Ruiz II and III. The cathedral was finally completed in 1776, by Juan de Ochoa. More than two centuries had passed since it began, and this explains the presence of so many subsequent styles, from the original Gothic to the Baroc and to the Neo-Classic.

From the ellipsoidal shape of the cathedral dome is suspended a majestic silver chandelier. The altar wall is in red marble, and is covered with old paintings. The chorus corner is the work of the 18th century sculptor Pedro Duque Cornejo.

Turn back to the orange tree courtyard, through the same door you came in; leave the Mezquita grounds at the **Puerta de Santa Catalina**. Follow the grounds wall to the left hand corner and unto Velázquez St. The first alley on your right is the **Calleja de las Flores** (Flowers' Alley);

THE MEZQUITA

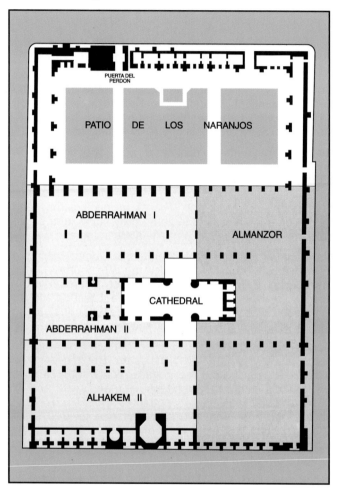

PUERTA DEL PERDON

PATIO DE LOS NARANJOS

ABDERRAHMAN I

ALMANZOR

ABDERRAHMAN II

CATHEDRAL

ALHAKEM II

the reason for the name is obvious. But the beauty of this alley is not only due to its flowers: it is also due to its setting, and to the way it frames the ancient belltower.

Back at the Mezquita corner, turn right into **Calle Judería** (Alley of the Jewish Quarter). Follow it

Cordoba — Moorish arches

Cordoba — the Alcázar Gardens

along the wall, to turn into Medina y Corella St. Then turn left into Manriquez St., which after a few paces opens into Plaza Yehuda Levi.

Manrique St. continues beyond the square, and the wide-open door of the second house on your right beckons you into an inner courtyard, with the entrances to several private residences on its sides. Looking around, you will see how refreshingly quiet it is, with all its potted plants and flowers, so inviting and clean. It is customary to leave a small donation after your visit.

From Manriquez St. proceed now to Maimonides St., following it back to the square, and then to **Calle Judíos** (Street of the Jews). On your left is Tiberias Square, with Maimonides' statue, recently erected to commemorate his eighth centenary. Maimonides (1135-1204) was a Jewish philosopher, whose work was very influential not only among the Jews, but also among Christians and Moslems of his and later times. Born in Cordoba, in 1148 he was persecuted and forced to leave. After years of wandering, he finally settled in Egypt. His memory is revered by the Jewish people to this day. Having crossed the square, a few more steps on Calle Judíos will bring you to the **Synagogue** (open Tuesday-Saturday, 10am-2pm and 4-7pm; Mondays 10am-2pm. Entrance fee).

The Synagogue was built in 1315, during the reign of King Alfonso XI. It is another instance of the unique climate of religious tolerance so frequent in Medieval Spain: here was a Christian King who had his Moslem builders erect a synagogue for his Jewish subjects...

The simple facade of the synagogue is belied by the splendour of its interior. The stucco arabesques on the walls are biblical quotes in the original Hebrew. Like elsewhere in Spain, this synagogue only survived since it was transformed into a church after the expulsion of the Jews from Spain in 1492. A few years after Franco's death, in the beginning of the 1980s, Spain was in the process of re-entering the family of nations, often through a re-examination and research of its own history. The Jewish contribution to the cultural life of ancient Spain was finally recognized and many ancient synagogues and other Jewish sites were accurately restored and declared national monuments.

Across the street from the synagogue you will find the wide courtyard of the old Jewish Market, today a nest of artists' studios and workshops.

Follow Calle Judíos to its upper end, and turning left you will come to **Puerta de Almodóvar**, the ancient Moorish gate of the Jewish Quarter. Beyond the gate, between the city and the Moorish walls (very well preserved in this sector), are the **Victoria Gardens**.

If you wish to spend some more time in Cordoba, there are several other interesting sites to see:

The **Alcázar de los Reyes Cristianos** is little more than a ruin, but its gardens are well worth a visit. Open 9.30am-1.30pm; summer afternoons 5-8pm and winter afternoons 4-7pm; entrance fee.

The **Palacio de Viana** is a splendid palace in the northern part of the city, with 14 courtyards, each with its own individual character; in the palace halls you will find an interesting exhibition of ancient furniture. Open 9am-2pm (in winter 10am-1pm) and 4-6pm; Sundays and holidays, mornings only. Entrance fee.

Less that 4 miles north-west of Cordoba you will come to **Medina Azahara** (a.k.a. Old Cordoba), with the 10th century palace of Caliph Abed-el-Rahman III and his beloved wife Zahara.

The whole town was destroyed in 1031 by the invading *Almorávides* tribes. The ruins cover a considerable area, and archaeological studies are under way, though very far from completion as of yet.

The local museum of ceramics, shards, tiles and other artifacts is open to visitors 10.30-12am; in summer afternoons 5.30-7pm and in winter afternoons 3.30-5pm.

Toward Malaga

Leave Seville toward the south-east on road N-334. After 9 miles you will reach **Alcal de Guadaria**, an old Roman strategic outpost. Here the Moors built a fortress, whose holders could dominate the Seville-Malaga Road. The white residential houses of the present town can be seen down the road, in the valley of the **Guadaira River**. The ruins of the watermills belong also to the Moorish period. The name of the town is also Arabic: *Al Kalat Guad-*

A "White Village"

Xira — The Valley-Floor Fortress. The town is famous for its many *Bariero* sandpits, the golden sand used to pave Seville's yellowish streets, long before the age of modern asphalt.

The next stop along N-334 will be **Osuna**.

Osuna

Osuna has a long and impressive past, as do most of the towns and villages of the region. The Iberian tribes of Southern Spain settled here, several thousand years ago, founding a trade and farming centre known as *Urso*. The name is mentioned in the chronicles of the war of succession between Pompeius and Julius Caesar. The Ursians were on Pompeius' side. The Moors named the town *Oxuna*; its main importance was, in those times, its strategic position on the Seville-Malaga Road. After the *Reconquista* (in 1239) the town became the capital of the small Girón family fief, created as a token of the King's gratitude for Girón's contribution to the war.

You are now about 60 miles east of Seville. Having stopped here, you might pay a short visit to the structures built by

Ronda — the Roman bridge

Pedro Téllez de Girón, founder of the Calatrava Order, and to the 15th century **Antigua Audiencia**, Palace of Justice; these are only two of several interesting palaces of the same epoch.

The **Colegiata** Church, high on top of the hill, is a **Museo del Arte Sacro** today, with several interesting paintings by José Ribera. The **Old University** (founded 1548) has a remarkable library and several beautiful large halls. The **Mausoleo Ducal**, near the old university, is the ducal family burial grounds.

Estepa

Only 7 miles east of Osuna is **Estepa**, a small centre with a population of 10,000 people. The settlement was populated without interruption by a long series of nations: the Iberians, the Carthaginians, the Romans, the Visigoths, the Moors and the *Reconquista* Spaniards. It is strategically situated high upon the hills, well above the Seville-Malaga Road, at a height of about 2,000 feet above sea level.

Its skyline is dominated by the **Torre de la Victoria**, a *Reconquista* period tower erected on Roman and Moorish foundations. From its top you will see a staggering view of the town and its surroundings. You will see the domes of several interesting churches around the tower, most of them in Baroc style.

Visit the beautiful **Palacio del Marqués de Cerverales**, whose impressive columns are known as *Columnas Salomónicas*. A second tower, the **Torre del Homenaje** was originally a palace sentry post. The town streets are pleasant and picturesque.

South of Seville

The "Pueblos Blancos"

In all of Spain, but specially in Andalusia, there are very many "Pueblos Blancos" (White Villages). Some are very small — just a handful of families — while others are sizable country towns. They are all very attractive and picturesque.

The road between **Jerez** and **Ronda** crosses the Sierra Sur mountains (whose highest peak, El Bosque, reaches more than 5000 feet a.s.l.), passing through several "White Villages". The hills around them, their meandering alleys and their white-washed walls, their women in black and their flowered window sills form a spectacular scenery reminiscent of a legendary, forgotten past.

Ronda

Ronda's bus stop is in the modern *Mercadillo*, on the north-western side of the dale.

Ronda was founded by the Romans, who called it *Arunda*, and has been for two millennia a very popular summer resort, where the city-dwellers find respite from the torrid summer of the plains.

Ronda is proud of its bullfight arena, one of the oldest. In fact, the bullfighting code still strictly honoured throughout Spain was redacted here in 1698. For almost a century the local Corridas were held regularly on Sundays in the town's main square, until in 1785, upon completion of the arena, they were transferred to their exclusive seat.

There is a spectacular observation point high on the boulder top, above a 500 feet almost perpendicular drop. At your left you will see the town, as if it were suspended above the abyss. Back at the arena, turn right. Beyond the square there is a Roman bridge, still used by the main road connecting the village to the coastal plain. Cross the bridge (a 130 feet archway above a 500 feet deep chasm) and you will find yourself at the gates of the old city.

Ronda's narrow and winding alleys are pleasant and attractive, but passing through you will also be able to admire some outstanding old buildings.

The Palacio del Marqués de Salvatiera is an impressive Renaissance residence, with beautifully decorated sills and balustrades. The Baños Arabes (Arab Baths) confirm the fact that even during the Moorish period Ronda was a popular summer resort. The Church of Santa María Mayor bears witness to its past as a Moorish Mosque, as well as the imprints of the Gothic and Renaissance styles. In its interior, the Moslem *Mihrab* can still be recognized by its Arabic inscriptions. The Mondragón Plaza was one of the summer residences of the Catholic Kings.

Now take the Jerez Road — whether by car or by bus, whose stop is on the main square. The Tourist Information Office is also there, on Plaza de España 1, tel. (952)871272.

From Ronda to Jerez

The road from Ronda to Jerez goes through a hilly woodland that has been partly declared as a National Park. Along the way you will come across several mountain villages, very attractive from afar, but rather disappointing when you reach them. Above the villages, higher up on the mountain slopes, you will see several old churches and castles. If you are travelling by bus, its brief stops

Ronda

El Rocío — the Pentecost festivities

will probably be sufficient to get an idea of most sites. If you wish to wander through the narrow mountain alleys of those villages, or to visit some of the neighbouring sites, you may wait for the next bus. But the best way to travel in this region is by private (or hired) car.

If you are on your own, in your car, we suggest a left hand turn at **Grazalema**, to the side road of Cadiz — through Uberique, Alcalá de los Gazules and Medina Sidonia where you may enjoy a livelier countryside. The buses reach Jerez on the main road, passing through Arcos de la Frontera.

Jerez

Jerez, 50 miles from Seville, is the last stop on this trip. It is a large town, with a population of about 180,000 people. After passing through the pastoral "White villages", Jerez appears as a large and bustling industrial city, somewhat disappointing in spite of its several interesting sites.

Jerez is famous mainly for its wines and horses — in that order. Probably its first wine-producers were the Romans. Jerez's wines (*Vinos de Jerez*) have a unique bitter-sweet aroma. On Jerez streets you will see many a *Bodega de Vinos*, some of which are open to visitors (for a fee) on workday mornings. During the visit, you will be also invited to sample some of the most recent vintages. There is a wide spectrum of Jerez wines, from the dryest to the mellowest: the sweet *Jerez Dulce*, the bitter *Jerez Quina*, the delicate *Jerez Fino* and the aromatic *Jerez Oloroso*. The harvest festival is in September.

Jerez's horses are perhaps not less famous than its wines. At the **Real Escuela Andaluza de Arte Ecuestre** (The Royal Andalusian School of Equestrian Art, Avenida Duque de Abrantes s/n, tel. 311111) there is every Thursday at 12.00 a weekly show of horsemanship on the best thoroughbred horses in the region. The April **Feria del Caballo** attracts thousands of horse-lovers and traders from all over the world.

The **Alcázar** of Jerez is but a ruin, and has little to distinguish it from other similar structures elsewhere in Andalusia. The full name of the town, "Jerez de la Frontera" (Frontera = Border) indicates that in early days the site was a strategical defensive fortress, a Catholic bastion against eventual Moorish incursions, not infrequent for almost two centuries after the 1264 Reconquista. The **Iglesia de Colegiata**, built on the ruins of the old great mosque, was twice restored in the 16th and 17th centuries.

The local Tourist Information Office is at 7 Alameda Cristina, tel. 331150 and 331162.

The Parque Nacional de Doñana

55 miles south-west of Seville, the Guadalquivir Delta swamps form a large parkland area of almost 200,000 acres. The visit to Doñana National Park requires a whole day, and it may be a rather complex enterprise. To protect park life, the number of daily visitors is strictly limited. A permit must be obtained from the National Parks Authority (tel. (955)430432) several days before the trip. If you were unable to obtain a permit, the Tourist Information Office (tel. 430086) may know of some organized tours. Using regular buses, take the Seville-Matalascañas or the Seville-El Rocío iines. Only the Parks Authority buses and four-wheel-drive vehicles are allowed entrance to the main park area. The best season is autumn. In summer, come prepared with some good insect-repellent and lots of drinking water. Closed on Monday.

The Park is famous for its delta quick-sands and swamp-land fauna: more than 250 species of birds and various species of mammals and rodents. At the entrance hut one may hire binoculars and buy selected literature and guides to the local fauna.

El Rocío

The village of Rocío is not far from the entrance to the park. According to a local legend, during the Moorish period some local Christian villagers hid a revered wooden statue of the Virgin Mary in the swamp. After the Reconquista the swamp returned the old statue to the townfolk, who placed it in the main chapel of the local church, where it is claimed to have performed many miraculous cures. It soon became famous, and on *Pentecostés* (Whitsunday) believeres flocked to the village church in their thousands. Many villagers have also found their own living in this legend, and a small industry of wooden replicas of the miraculous statue and other religious objects has become one of the village's most profitable enterprises.

Aracena — The cave of the Marvels

Aracena is 55 miles north-west of Seville, in the heart of the Sierra Morena Mountains. It is a pleasant, cool mountain village, whose major attraction is the **Gruta de las Maravillas** (Cave of the Marvels). The cave was discovered accidentally by a boy while he was searching for a missing pig. It is the largest stalagtite grotto in Spain, and has some spectacular halls and passages. Visitors are led in groups of 10-15 persons by professional guides (fluent in several foreign languages). It is open daily, June-September 9am-7pm and the rest of the year 10am-6pm. The groups form every two hours on the hour, but on your arrival you will do well to inquire about eventual timetable changes.

After the visit to the Grotto you may stop also at the **Iglesia del Castillo**, a beautiful Mudéjar-Gothic structure built by the Templars upon the ruins of an old Moorish fortress. El Rocío is a good starting point for several interesting mountain walks and car excursions, and it has also several small but pleasant hotels.

SEVILLE

Making the Most of Your Stay

Andalusian Cuisine

The Capital of Andalusia is also a major culinary center. A leisurely meal at one of its best restaurants will not only satisfy your appetite, it will also provide your plate with an unforgettable experience. Even in the simplest inns of the poorer suburbs, Seville's brand is undoubtedly the best of all Andalusian kitchens.

The fundamentals of Andalusian cuisine are more or less typically Spanish: the main staples are *vaca* (beef), *jamón* (pork) and *huevos* (eggs). In spite of its distance from the sea, Seville also offers an abundant selection of seafood (*mariscos*) and fish (*pescado*). And whatever you order, you will get a plateful fit for a giant's belly. Filling — and rather heavy.

Now a word about the spices. Seville's cooks are rather heavy-handed, and all their best dishes send a rich caleidoscopic bouquet to your nose and tongue, at first it will surprise you, but later you probably will not want to do without it.

Most respectable meals begin with a *gazpacho*, a cold, spicy soup, made to order for Sevillan summers. The ingredients of the soup came from the New World: *tomates*, *pepinos* (cucumbers), *ajo* (garlic), *pimientos* (peppers). Together with the *pan* (bread), *aceite* (oil), *vinagre* and *sal*, they make a hell of a good soup.

There are several other interesting entrées: *huevos a la flamenca* (a baked concoction of eggs, tomatoes, onions, garlic and mixed spices), *cabrillas* (large pasture snails) and *caracoles* (little, white garden snails).

The most common main dish is the *paella sevillana*, stewed seafood on a bed of rice. But the pièce de résistance, not surprisingly in the heart of corrida-land, is *cola de toro* — oxtail in a heavy wine sauce.

For variety's sake, one may order a *caldereta* (beef in wine sauce and spices), *carne con tomate* (beef and tomatoes) or *ternera a la sevillana* (veal in a cherry and olives spicy sauce). The commonest side dish is *espinaca con carbanzo* (spinach and chick-peas).

For a quick take-away snack you may choose between *pescadito frito* (a paper bag full of small fried fish — but no chips...) and *tapas*, a local speciality worth a special paragraph of its own (see below).

Do you have a sweet-tooth? For desserts, you will enjoy the local nunneries' specialities, *yemas de San Leandro* or *bollitos de Santa Inés*, both rich in eggs and sugar content. Slightly lighter are the *mostachones* (homemade wine pastries) and the *biscocho borracho* (biscuit with rum).

During the *Holy Week* Sevillans stuff themselves with *tortitas* (fried cakes made of bread, wine, eggs and honey) and *pestiños* (fried cakes made of flour, water, lemon juice and honey).

Seville's Restaurants

Such an old aristocratic capital as Seville must offer a wide and rich selection of good restaurants.

Breakfast here, in general, is no big deal. Some of the larger tourists' hotels may boast a buffet table, but in most cases you will probably find very little to write home about. Lunch hour is 2.30-4.30pm, but many restaurants commence serving at 12.30am. At 4.30pm they close. They re-open for dinner, at 8pm, and serve until midnight, or even later.

Sevillan restaurants are among the most expensive in Spain. The following list is divided in four categories:

Very expensive: over US$ 120 for two.
Expensive: US$ 80-120 for two.
Moderately-priced: US$ 40-80 for two.
Inexpensive: under US$ 40 for two.

The prices are for three-course dinners, with simple wines or soft beverages. Vintage vines are very expensive. There is also a 6% tax — and your waiter will expect a 10% tip. Credit cards (*VISA, Eurocard, American Express, Diner's* etc.) are welcome in most good restaurants.

Nobody dresses for lunch, but many restaurants require formal dress for dinner. If in doubt, you will do well to inquire while you call to reserve your table. Dinner is lengthy and leisurely, a two hour affair at least. Beware of the ever-present TV set: most Spaniards eat to the accompaniment of vintage horror films, while the innocent bystanders may find such a diet too heavy for comfort.

Very expensive restaurants

Itálica: 2 calle San Fernando, tel. 422-2850, in the exclusive *Alfonso XIII Hotel*. The most expensive restaurant in the most expensive hotel. Reservations and formal dress a must. International "Five Forks" cuisine.

El Burladero: 1 Calle Canalejas, tel. 421-3270, in the *Tryp Colón Hotel*. International cuisine and first class cellar. Reservations and formal dress.

La Dehesa: Calle Luis de Morales, tel. 457-9400, in the *Hotel los Lebreros*. Very good Andalusian cuisine. Reservations and formal dress.

Expensive restaurants

La Albahaca: 12 Plaza Santa Cruz, tel. 422-0714. An expensive but very popular restaurant; traditional Andalusian cuisine. In an impressive old palace in the heart of Santa Cruz. Recommended. Reservations.

Maitres: 54 Avenida República Argentina, tel. 445- 6880. In the fashionable Los Remedios neighbourhood. Traditional Andalusian cuisine. Reservations. Closed on Sunday.

Cambados: 12 Calle Uruguay, tel. 461-600. A good restaurant in the relaxed Heliopolis neighbourhood. Excellent Galician cuisine and sea-food. Reservations.

Antares: 7 Genaro Parladé, tel. 462-7551. Incomparable Basque cuisine in the Maria Luisa Park. Reservations. Closed on Sunday and for lunch on Saturday. Good selection of game.

La Isla: 25 Arfe, tel. 421-5376. A popular restaurant with a sample of different Spanish regional foods. Warmly recommended for its pies and fish. Closed in August. Reservations.

San Marco: 6 Cuna, tel. 421-2440. A picturesque restaurant in an old historic setting. Cheaper than most others in its class. Closed in August and on Sunday. Reservations.

Egaña Oriza: 41 San Fernando, tel. 422-7211. Good Basque cuisine; opposite the University. Reservations.

_Ox's_: 61 Betis, tel. 427-9585. A pleasant restaurant run by the owners of the _Egaña Oriza_; same Basque cuisine, intimate atmosphere. Open also for business lunches. Reservations.

L'Arroz: 6 Juan Antonio Cavestany, tel. 441-9103. A modern restaurant, specializing in various Valencia rice recipes. Very good pies. Relatively inexpensive.

La Dorada: 6 Virgen de Aguas Santas, tel. 445-0220. Excellent sea-food restaurant, with a branch at 16 Calle José Luis de Casso (tel. 445-5100). Reservations; closed on Sunday and in August.

Rio Grande: 70 Betis, tel. 427-3956. It has lost some of its former fame, but carries still the exceptional appeal of a good Andalusian dinner served on a terrace with the best view in town.

El Figón del Cabildo: Plaza del Cabildo, tel. 422-0117. An elegant but relatively expensive place; regional Spanish food. Very central, not far from the Cathedral. Reservations; closed on Sunday.

Florencin: 49 Avenida Eduardo Dato, tel. 457-0040, in the _Porta Coeli Hotel_. Good enough to be frequented by most local businessmen. International cuisine. Reservations and formal dress.

Moderately-priced restaurants

Corral del Agua: 6 Callejon del Agua. Authentic Spanish cuisine under the Alcázar walls.

Bodegón Torre del Oro: 15 Calle Santander, tel. 421-4241. A spacious restaurant, often selected by many tourist guides for their American groups, to introduce them to various Spanish regional cuisines. One of the rare places open from 7am to 1am.

San Francisco: 10 Plaza San Francisco, tel. 422-2056. Situated in a very attractive old residence. Serves French-Spanish dishes, with an outstanding selection of local wines. Near the City Hall; relatively expensive. Reservations. Closed Sunday night and all Monday.

El Bacalao: 15 Plaza Ponce de Léon, tel. 421-6670. Specializes in _bacalau_ (cod), the popular staple of the Portuguese and Spanish Atlantic Coast. Closed on Sunday.

Bodegón el Riojano: 12 Virgen de las Montañas, tel. 445-

0682. In the Los Remedios neighbourhood. Impressive arched ceilings; frequented by the best local society. Traditional Andalusian; reservations.

Asador Jugopan: 42 Calle San Eloy, tel. 456-0629. A good *asado* (roast) restaurant in the very centre of town. Reservations.

La Cueva: 18 Rodrigo Caro, tel. 421-3143. In the heart of Santa Cruz; famous for its lamb recipes. Pleasant open-air tables on the square, with street-musicians and singers. Friendly atmosphere; reasonably priced.

Luna Parque: 1 Avenida María Luisa, tel. 423-2414. A large restaurant in the Maria Luisa Park. Tasty and inexpensive Andalusian food; excellent oxtail. Weekend flamenco evening performances. Reservations a must on flamenco nights.

El Barranco: 12 Arjona, tel. 422-2080. Good Spanish and international cuisine on the riverside, near the Isabel II Bridge. Reservations; closed on Sunday.

Mesón Puerta de Jerez: 6 Maese Rodrigo, tel. 422-9890. A small, intimate inn in a typical 19th century Sevillan residence. Outstanding *gazpacho* and sea-food recipes. Reservations; closed on Sunday.

El Giraldillo: 2 Plaza Virgen de los Reyes, tel. 421-4525. Uniquely situated opposite the cathedral and the Giralda. A characteristic tourists' restaurant, serving slightly domesticated Spanish food. Reservations.

Casa Robles: 58 Alvarez Quintero, tel. 421-3150. An old, central restaurant serving the best oxtail in town. Perfect for a first encounter with Sevillan food.

Hostería del Laurel: 5 Plaza de los Venerables, tel. 422-0295. In one of the best spots in Santa Cruz. Very pleasant view from the open-air tables. Picturesque rural decorations. Spanish and international cuisines.

Inexpensive restaurants

Los Alcázares: 10 Miguel de Mañara, tel. 421-3103. The right place for a very good and inexpensive Andalusian dinner in Santa Cruz; try its *gazpacho*, and as a main course, the *paella sevillana*. Closed on Sunday.

Las vegas: 7 Alemanes, tel. 421-3145. A small, pleasant pie-house, with pleasant sidewalk tables.

Buffet el Diamante: 11 Avenida de la Constitución. A *buffet libre* (self-service buffet) restaurant, opposite the Cathedral. Good for a large, inexpensive (less than US$

10 per person) meal; buffet served until 7.30pm. There is also a slightly more expensive branch on Alemanes St.

There are many other relatively inexpensive restaurants; you will find several of them along Mateos Gago St., East of the Giralda. Several are Spanish places, others Italian, and a few are Chinese. The street itself is crowded but pleasant unto the small hours of the night.

Tapas

Tapas are the ideal solution for a casual, cheap and filling snack. They are served in several restaurants, but mostly in the *tapas* bars and kiosks. *Tapa* in Spanish means "cover", and it is meant here in the sense that it "covers your appetite".

Tapas is served in small plates; each plate is a serving. It is best to start with two or three, proceeding then with additional orders, until your appetite is duly "covered". *Tapas* vary from place to place, but in general they contain minute fried fish and other seafood or snails. You will indicate your own preference, and you will pay according to the number of servings consumed. The final price will remain considerably lower than that of a regular meal.

Some of the best known *tapas* bars are:
Casa Roman: Plaza de los Venerables, in Santa Cruz.
Bar Giralda: Calle Mateos Gago, near the Cathedral.
Kiosko de las Flores: Calle Betis, on the western bank of the river.
El Reconcillo: 40 Calle Gerona.
Sol y Sombra: Calle Castilla.
Las Teresas: Calle Santa Teresa.

The wines of Andalusia

The local taverns, called *bodega* or *tasca*, serve a variety of alcoholic beverages, *bocadillos* (sandwiches) and often also *tapas*. They are very well frequented specially just before dinner time, when lots of people step in for a bracing glass of wine on the way to a restaurant. It may also be convenient to drop in at other times, and even in the late hours of the night you will find in most *bodegas* the makings of a cheap, simple last "cover" before bedtime.

Wine is drawn straight from the barrel. Even in the most

modest *bodegas* you will have the choice of at least four or five varieties; in the more pretentious locals the whole back wall of the place is lined with scores of barrels containing different brands. Prices are reasonable, and the atmosphere is relaxed and friendly.

Local wines are very popular; there is the Montilla (near Cordoba) produced *Amontillado* ; there are the various types of *Jerez*: the *Manzanilla* (rather sweet but very delicate), the *Oloroso* (old, thick and very sweet), the *Mosto* (very young and aggressive). Some taverns make it a point to also keep less popular varieties, like the very sweet *Jerez Dulce* or the really bitter *Jerez Quina*, laced with quinin.

Every restaurant has at least a few simple brands of table wine: *tinto* (red), *blanco* (white), or *rosado* (rosé); the simplest and cheapest is generally the *vino de la casa* (wine of the house); it also fits in very well with local menus. Most restaurants will also serve some of the more expensive *Rioja* wines, that come from the Ebro valley vineyards. The *Rioja* are connoisseur's wines, and the choice among their different varieties requires a certain expertise; you will do well to vary your choice according to the occasion. Spaniards love to drink, and their wines are gradually gaining increasing international recognition.

The best and most expensive restaurants in town are equipped with vast cellars, where they also keep some of the best Catalonian, French and Portuguese brands.

Shopping

In spite of its modest size, Seville is a very pleasant place to shop in. It has a variety of shops and stores; your English will be more or less accurately grasped practically everywhere — and most shopkeepers have very good, smiling counter-side manners.

Don't forget that air-conditioning is still almost unknown in Sevillan shops, and that they close at lunchtime for a longish siesta. Toward sunset, when the air cools down, the shops fill up with prospective buyers. If you have the markets' bug — don't forget to bargain with apparent authority — most market peddlers only expect to get a fraction of their first asking price from their buyers.

Where to shop for what

It may be assumed that toward the end of your stay you will want to shop for souvenirs and small presents to take home. There is a vast variety of *abanicos* (hand fans — good also for daily use during your stay): some are Taiwan made in plastics, others are locally made in black, delicate lace...

Among other local specialities we will mention *cerámicas* (pots), *azulejos* (coloured tiles), and the famous Andalusian shawls: the larger ones are called *mantones*, the smaller version is the *mantilla*. Then there are the flamboyant red and black flamenco outfits, with their smaller, more modest attachments — the *castañuelas*.

There are scores of antiquarian stores (*antigüedades*); their merchandise — mostly old religious art objects — may be authentic, or replicas or forgeries. For the more practical-minded there are many *orfebrerías* (silver- and goldsmiths), where local and country artisans sell their almost millennary traditional jewellery. Then there are the gorgeous *bordados en oro* (gold lace), a centuries old trade whose secrets are passed on from mother to daughter in the mountains.

The Avenida de la Constitución is lined with gift and tourists' shops: they offer plenty of printed T-shirts, sunhats, ashtrays, pens — and also more "serious" stuff, like old bottled ships and other curios. Sierpes St., Los Remedios and Santa Cruz are the main shopping areas in town, with some of the best shops.

Antigüedades
Segundo Antigüedades: 89 Sierpes, tel. 422-5652.
Lola Ortega: 4 Plaza del Cabildo, tel. 421-8771.
Andres Moro: 8 Placentines, tel. 422-4623.
Felix e Hijos: 20-26 Avenida de la Constitución, tel. 422-3334.
Altamira: 7 Rodrigo Caro, tel. 421-6558.
Vélez Melchor: 10 Plaza de Santa Cruz, tel. 421-2228.

Arts and Crafts (*Artesanía*)
Artespaña: 2 Plaza de la Concordia, tel. 422-1865. Art objects from all Spain.
Populart: 4 Pasaje de Vila, tel. 422-9444. In Santa Cruz.
Alcuza: 3 Virgen de Regla, tel. 427-3797. In Los Remedios.

Fans (*Abanicos*)
Casa Rubio: 56 Sierpes, tel. 422-6872.

Shawls (*Mantones, Mantillas*)
Feliciano Foronda: 52 Alvarez Quintero, tel. 422-9148. Lace specialists.

Traditional Costumes (*Trajes Tipicos*)
Lina: 7 Lineros, tel. 421-2423.
Celis: 14 Plaza de San Francisco, tel. 421-3141.
Pardales: 23 Cuna, tel. 421-3709.
Creaciones Rincón: 35 Monte Carmelo, in Los Remedios, tel. 427-4372.

Pots and Pans (*Cerámica y Alfarería*)
Santa Cruz: 10 Mateos Gago, tel. 422-6896.
Martian: 74 Sierpes, tel. 421-3413.
Taller Aguilas: 25 Aguilas, tel. 421-1626.
Cerámica Santa Ana: 31 San Jorge, tel. 433-3990.

Silver and Goldsmiths (*Orfebrerías*)
Marmolejo Hernández: 2 Avenida Eduardo Dato, tel. 457-6025.

Orfebrería Triana: 66 Pureza, tel. 427-3765.

Traditional Hats (*Sombrerías***)**
Maquedano: 40 Sierpes.
Espinosa: 2 San Isidro.

Gold Lace (*Bordados en Oro***)**
José Carrasquilca Perea: 36 San Luis.
Martin Cruz: Don Pedro Niño.
Esperanza Ellena Caro: Jesús del Gran Poder.

Department Stores
The larger stores are air-conditioned, and remain open throughout the day.

El Corte Inglés: 10 Plaza del Duque de la Victoria, tel. 422-0931.
Galerías Preciados: 1 San Pablo, tel. 422-2961 and 422-2014.

Books (*Librerías***)**
Cervantes: 35 San Fernando, tel. 422-9328.
Girardillo: 17 San Fernando, tel. 422-8643.
Librería Pasquallazaro: 4 Sierpes — with a rich selection of English books and albums about Spain.

Markets
The largest Market (*El Jueves*) is open on Thursday on Calle de la Feria, in the north of town, east of Alameda de Hércules. It is a market with all sorts of merchandise; prices are considerably lower than in regular shops. Rich selections of toys and ceramics. Some interesting old objects may sometimes be discovered, hidden among tons of junk.

Other smaller markets are open on Sunday. We have already mentioned the *Mercadillo Filatélico* of Plaza del Cabildo, the Pet Market of Plaza de Alfalfa and the Flea Market of Alameda de Hércules. They are lively and picturesque. Once again, they operate only on Sunday mornings, and close soon after lunchtime.

Nightlife

The most popular evening entertainment is a leisurely restaurant dinner, or a simpler *tapas* meal. Then there are the traditional "strolling grounds" in the centre — along Sierpes St., in Santa Cruz or Los Remedios. If you wish to join the crowd, however, beware of unlit streets and other dark corners.

The *Teatro de la Maestranza*, not far from the centre of town on the riverside, has a repertory of operas and ballets productions. The *Lope de Vega* Theatre, situated at the entrance of the Maria Luisa Park, offers programmes of songs and dance.

Plays are produced only in Spanish; most films are also dubbed in Spanish. To avoid unnecessary disappointments, inquire before buying your tickets.

Flamenco

The most popular tourist attraction is provided by the several *Tablaos* (Flamenco Halls), where one may enjoy the unique flavour of *Sevillanas*. These dramatic Flamenco productions highlight the daily life of Andalusia peasants in dance, song and music (see part one, "Culture and arts — music and dance"). One does not have to be fluent in Spanish to catch the motives, to absorb the tunes, and to feast one's eyes in the dance. The *Tablao* is like a theatre hall, with rows of rather uncomfortable seats (no tableside show!); if possible, bring your own pillow. The programme lasts for ninety minutes, and the tickets cost more than US$ 30. The best *Tablaos* are:

Los Gallos: 11, Plaza de Santa Cruz, tel. 422-8522. One of the oldest and most respected, active for more than 25 years. Folkloristic overtones. In the heart of Santa Cruz.

El Patio Sevillano: 11a Paseo Cristóbal Colón, tel. 421-4120. Two main halls and two richly decorated inner courtyards, very close to the *Maestranza* arena. Frequented by many tourist groups, its size and box-office hits ensure the highest standards of its performers.

El Arenal: 7 Rodo, tel. 421-6492. In an old 17th century palace, situated between the *Maestranza* Arena and theatre. High standards traditional flamenco topped by modern improvisations. Recommended.

For those who don't appreciate the formal atmosphere of the *Tablaos*, there are occasional Flamenco shows in the crowded tourist centres in town, especially on weekend evenings, in Santa Cruz or along Calle Sierpe. Some of the smaller restaurants and clubs of Calle Salado, in fashionable Los Remedios, also offer side shows of Flamenco.

The night Guadalquivir cruises are also a spectacular form of entertainment. The most refined motor-cruiser is the *El Patio* (tel. 421-3836 during office hours; nights (908)150051). Its cruises include a Flamenco show, a glass of *Sangría* wine and other Spanish attractions. The cruise starts at 11.15pm and lasts until midnight. Other motor-boats offer dinner cruises with adequate bar services. For information, call *Barco Lola*, tel. 462-7448 or *Sevillana de Cruleros*, tel. 421-1396.

For a quiet evening on the riverside, make your own choice among the bars and restaurants that line the river on both banks between the Golden Tower and the Isabel II Bridge. Some of them have open-air tables, others have wide windowed terraces opening toward the river.

A spicy flavour of adventure is available to those who'd like to slum in the dark taverns of the Macarena neighbourhood, on Feria, San Luis and Castellar Sts. It is not one of the best areas in town; it is advisable not to come on your own.

The Cathedral and the Giralda keep their night lighting on until 11pm. The pleasant café on Plaza Virgen de los Reyes is perfect to enjoy the view. For even more spectacular sights one may hire a coach ride from the Alcázar walls to Plaza España. Avoid the Maria Luisa Park at night.

Sports
Seville is too aristocratic-minded to let itself go and enjoy the intense sport life of larger cities, such as Madrid or Barcelona. Soccer is still the most popular sport, thanks to

Seville's two reputable clubs. The better one, *Seville F.C.*, plays at the *Sanchez Pizjuan* stadium, on Luis Morales St.; the second, *Betis*, plays at the *Benito Villamarin* stadium, in the southern suburbs. The soccer season begins in October and ends in April; detailed information is available in the dailies.

Only very few hotels are equipped with tennis courts or other sport facilities. Tennis buffs will find what they are looking for at the *Piscinas Sevillas* (81 Avenida Ciudad Jardín, tel 463-5892) or at the *Piscina Municipal Virgen de los Reyes* (Avenida Doctor Fepriani, s/n, tel. 437-6866); after their games, they will be able (for a reasonable fee) to jump in for a refreshing swim at one of the local pools (*Piscina* means in Spanish "swimming pool").

Near San Telmo Bridge, across the river from the Golden Tower, there are rowboats for hire.

EXPO '92

The inauguration ceremony of EXPO '92 was on Easter Monday, 20 April 1992. This great international show is meant to illustrate international achievements in the fields of science and technology all over the world. It is one of the vastest European enterprises in recent years, second only to the English channel tunnel.

The tradition of international fairs was born in the Middle Ages, when they represented almost the only opportunity open to traders, bankers and farmers desiring to meet and exchange their fares from land to land and from region to region. Fairs and Market days were also a day of rejoicing and revelry, and a unique source of culture, information and gossip exchanges between faraway lands. This is how new fashions travelled from land to land, and how new ideas could begin to circulate. The World Exhibition is in fact a gigantic oldtime fair, still popular and lively even in the age of fax and TV.

The World Exhibition of Christal Palace in London, 1851, was the first in a series of modern international fairs. All nations of the world were invited. Its success was tremendous. It created a first contact between different civilizations born in five continents. It was the showcase of Victorian Britain in all its splendour. After London, Paris hosted five consecutive world fairs between 1855 and 1900. The greatest was, of course, the 1089 Fair, on the Centennial of the French Revolution. Its major monument is the Eiffel Tower.

The international fairs industry grew soon after 1900, until it became necessary to set up an international steering committee, the *Bureau International des Exhibitions*, whose function is to coordinate projects and to avoid unnecessary and damaging competition. Then the idea of "sectorial" fairs was born, like the British Commonwealth Fair, the Ibero-American Spanish Fair — or the 1986 Transportation Fair of Vancouver (Canada).

Universal fairs are gigantic enterprises, and therefore not too frequent: in the last half-century there were only three: the Bruxelles Fair of 1958, the Montréal Fair of 1968, and the greatest of all, the Osaka (Japan) Fair of 1970, with 77 National Pavillions and almost 65 million visitors. And now we have Seville.

Why Seville? Each and every World Fair is meant to present and promote the achievements of the hosting country and city. The Bruxelles 1958 Fair stressed the reconstruction of Europe after the Second World War, and made Bruxelles the unofficial capital of Europe. Montréal and Osaka focussed the eyes of the world on those two great countries, emerging to new positions of world leadership. Spain had been one of the most backward countries in Europe for almost a century. Then, after Franco's death, the miracle. In less than a decade, Spain became a full-fledged member of Europe, competing successfully with the most advanced among European industrial nations. Once again, like in the Age of Discovery, Spain is a universal centre of human endeavours.

The choice of Seville as the seat of EXPO '92 has its roots in history. As the departure point of Columbus' voyages, Seville is the first direct link between Europe and the New World. Moreover, Spain, like other European countries, has its own "Deep South" development problems. Andalusia, one of Spain's most populous regions, is also one of its poorest, with the highest unemployment rate in the whole country. The gigantic EXPO '92 investment provided the means for urban growth, industrial development and prosperity throughout the region — and specially for Seville itself.

The date, of course, determines the fair's main theme: the fifth centennial of the Discovery of America. The *Age of Discovery* topics of the fair include five centuries of human progress in all scientific and technologic fields. Being so close to the end of our century, it is only natural that special attention be given also to man's expectations for the next; this attention finds suitable expression in a specially conceived pavillion.

La Cartuja
For the first time in the history of world fairs, the event will

take place in an historical setting intimately connected with the fair's main subject. The artificial La Cartuja island, enclosed on the western side of the city between the Guadalquivir River and the Alfonso XIII Canal, is at comfortable walking distance from the city centre and from most Sevillan main architectural and cultural gems.

The ancient **Monasterio Santa María de las Cuevas**, in the heart of La Cartuja, belonged originally to the Chartreuse Order founded in the 11th century in Grénoble (France) in the 11th century by St. Bruno. Cartuja is the Spanish translation of "Chartreuse". The local soil has been known for centuries as the best prime material for various types of earthenware and ceramics, and was mined and used as such as early as the Moorish period. This is how the zone became riddled with caves (in Spanish *Cuevas*). In one of those caves, in the 13th century, according to a popular legend the Virgin Mary appeared miraculously to her believers. In 1400, on that very site, Archbishop Gonzalo de Mena y Vargas built a new monastery in the characteristic Gothic-Mudéjar style. The building was frequently damaged so seriously, that its monks were repeatedly forced to abandon it until it could be suitably restored. Those restoration works are responsible for its Renaissance and Baroc appearance.

The Monastery of Santa María de las Cuevas was very dear to Christopher Columbus, who lived in its premises for several years and used its chapel for his daily devotions. Nobody knows how Columbus' love for this Monastery began, but after his second voyage the great explorer became a regular resident of Las Cuevas, and obtained spiritual guidance, support and even financial help from the Monastery monks and treasurers. Gaspar de Goricio, a monk also born in faraway Italy, became Columbus' confessor and faithful aide. Many of Columbus' letters are addressed to him — almost as many as those addressed to his own son (the correspondence is exhibited at the Seville Archivo de Indias). Don Gaspar was also the editor of at least three of Columbus' books, and the trusted keeper of all Columbus' documents and diaries.

Columbus died and was buried in Valladolid in 1506. His remains, however, were exhumed and transferred three years later to the Santa Anna Chapel of the Monastery.

There they remained until 1536, and in 1544 they were brought to Santo Domingo. What happened later is not clear, and many historians claim that the remains buried in the Seville cathedral are not really Columbus'. The monastery continued, after the explorer's death, to serve as the Columbus family's burial grounds. Christopher's brother, Don Diego, was buried there in 1515, his son Diego in 1526 and his grandson, Admiral Don Luis Columbus, in 1572. This intimate relationship was broken in 1609 by Don Nuño Columbus, heir of Christopher's nobiliar title, who removed all family documents from the monasterial archives.

The Monastery reapears in the annals of history in 1810, when the invading French forces used it as their high command post until their 1812 retreat. In 1835 the Monastery as such ceased to exist, and in 1841 the liberal Government of Spain confiscated its grounds and transformed its main building into a large ceramics factory, that was sold to Charles Pickman, a British industrialist. The factory was operational until 1982, when it was finally transferred to a modern site in the suburbs. The Monastery grounds were reappropriated by the state, and subsequently restored.

During EXPO '92 the Monastery houses three large exhibitions: **The Fifteenth Century Pavillion**, with an outstanding audio-visual programme dedicated to the Age of Discovery; the **1492 Hall of World Art and Culture** — the spectrum of the various cultures as seen from contemporary eyes: European, Byzantine, Islamic, Pre-Columbian, African and Far-Eastern; and **La Cartuja 1400-1992**, an exhibition of the monastery treasures and documented history.

EXPO '92 Investments and Settings

The scale of EXPO '92 works is simply gigantic. Much more than the originally planned US$ 7 billion were invested in the project. The whole interurban road network was extensively developed and expanded, and today Seville can be reached from all Europe through the network of the major continental highways. A special, supermodern train connects Seville directly with Madrid. Andalusian airports, railway stations and other facilities have been restored and expanded as much as possible. Seven new bridges have been drawn across the Guadalquivir and more than 100 pavillions have been erected on the fair grounds. 350,000 shrubs and trees of 400 different species have been planted in the EXPO '92 gardens. Many of the most prominent city buildings have been restored; several have been actually rebuilt from scratch. The number of hotel beds has been trebled in only two years. Indeed, a comprehensive, vertiginous, revolutionary metamorphosis.

General tourist information for accommodation

Two major Information Centres have been set up to assist the thousands of incoming tourists:

Coral (Centro oficial de Reservas de Alojamiento): tel. (95)429-0092. The official EXPO '92 Centre.

City of Welcome: tel. (95)428-493641. Room, hostel and pension information.

How to get there

Seville's, Malaga's and Jerez's airports have been prepared for the great event. The new Santa Justa railway station was inaugurated in 1991. There are parking facilities for 30,000 private vehicles, hundreds of special buses and scores of river-cruise motorboats. Day after day 250,000 visitors enter the fair grounds from its six gates. All possible steps have been taken to prevent or at least minimize the danger of traffic jams. A special helicopter service is available (at a considerable price) for those who land out of town.

Tickets

Entrance tickets are valid for all pavillions and shows. They are on sale at the six entrance gates and in all branches of the following banks: *Banco Español de Crédito, Banco Central, Banco Hispano-Americano, Banco Bilbao-Vizcaya.*

Prices

Daily tickets (9.00-4.00a.m.):
Adults: 4000 ptas.
Above 65 and children 5-14: 1500ptas.
Under 5 — entrance free.

Family days
Once or twice a month a 50% discount is offered to visiting families.

Single night tickets (20.00-04.00) — 1000ptas.

Cumulative tickets
3 day ticket — 10,000ptas.
Permanent ticket — 30,000ptas; half price for visitors above 65 or 5-14.
Permanent night ticket — 10,000ptas.

EXPO '92 in numbers
Area: 538 acres.
Floorspace: 100 acres.
Parking Spaces: 30,000.
Pavillions: more than 100.
Participant States more than 100; also more than 20 international organisations (United Nations, Red Cross etc.), and 17 Spanish regional administrations.
Duration: 176 days: 20 April 1992 — 12 October 1992.
Expected number of visitors: 18 million (55% Spaniards and the rest from abroad).
Daily number of visitors: 250,000.
Total number of visits: 40 million.
New roads built in the grounds: 25 miles.
Entrance Gates: 4 for motor vehicles, 2 pedestrian crossings, one railway gate.
New Guadalquivir Bridges: 7.
Restaurants: 105.
Pubs and cafeterias: 38.
Shops: 105.

The Programme
EXPO '92 presents the achievements of science and technology in modern, sophisticated media. Each state has the opportunity to exhibit its features in the best possible way. The different pavillions find themselves in continuous competition for the public's praise and interest. The pavillions of the Great Powers are particularly attractive; some represent an investment of hundreds of millions of dollars.

The French pavillion is based on space technology. The Swiss pavillion is crowned by a tall paper tower; the British pavillion's front is in transparent crystal, decorated by a 50 feet high waterfall; the Mexican pavillion is an exact replica of an Aztec pyramid; the Guatemalan pavillion is a "time tunnel" to the Mayan culture.

Four great pavillions are period settings: three are dedicated to the past — and one to the future. Here you are invited to experience a meteors' rain, to travel into a "black hole" etc.

The cultural experience is simply fantastic; in addition to what you will see in the Pavillions, you are invited to all sorts of music concerts, to plays, dances and other spectacles. All the grandest names of the performing arts are represented: the New York's Metropolitan Opera, La Scala of Milan, the London Royal Ballet, the Opera of Vienna, the Berlin Philarmonic Orchestra and many others. Among Spanish performers — the Flamenco Dancers of *Cristina Hoyos*, and the Cataloñan Ballet of *La Fura del Baus*.

Hundreds of the best classical motion pictures are shown on a gigantic 1000 square feet screen; each month is dedicated to different subjects: tragedy, passion, fantasy, etc. There are also hundreds of screenings of avant-garde films and performances of street-artists. It is a non-stop festival of all the arts, in a unique atmosphere set in the picturesque background of Seville.

Useful Addresses and Phone Numbers

Seville's area code: 95.
Spain's international code: 34.

Emergencies
Police: tel. 091.
Fire Brigade: tel. 080.
Red Cross: tel. 435-0135.
Ambulance: tel. 433-0993.
Hospital *Dispensario*: tel. 435-1400.

Tourist Information
Regional Tourist Office: Avenida de la Constitución, tel. 422-1404.
City Tourist Office: Paseo de las Delicias, s/n, tel. 423-4465.
Airport Tourist Office: tel. 425-5046.
EXPO '92 Tourist Office: tel. 446-1992.

Transportation
RENFE Railways: tel. 441-4111; for informations, tel. 442-1562.
Urban Buses: tel. 441-7111 and 441-7300.
Teletaxi: tel. 462-2222.
Radiotaxi: tel. 458-0000.
Radio Teléfono Taxi: tel. 435-9835.
Iberia Airlines: 3 Almirante Lobo, tel. 422-8901.

Miscellanea
International telephone calls: 2 Plaza Nueva.
Direct international dialling: 07.
International Telegrammes: tel. 422-6860.
Central Post Office (*Correo Central*): 32 Avenida de la Constitución, tel. 422-8800.
Lost and found: tel. 421-2800 and 421-5694.
Area directory information: tel. 003.
Inter-urban directory information: Target Area Code + 03.
Weather information: recorded message at tel. 094.
News headlines: recorded information at tel. 095.
Sports news: recorded information at tel. 097.

SEVILLE

U.S.A. Consulate: 7 Paseo de las Delicias, tel. 423-1885.
British Consulate: 8 Plaza Nueva, tel. 422-8875.
German Consulate: Av. R. de Carranza, 22, tel. 445-7811.
Danish Consulate: Av. Reina Mercedes, 25, tel. 461-1489.
Swedish Consulate: Av. Reina Mercedes, 25, tel. 461-1489.

Dictionary

English	Spanish	English	Spanish
good morning	*buenos días*	bus station	*parada del autobus*
hello / good bye	*hola, adiós*	train	*tren*
good evening	*buenas tardes*	subway	*metro*
good night	*buenas noches*	railway station	*estación de tren*
please	*por favor*	ticket	*billete*
thank you	*gracias*	taxi	*taxi*
pardon, excuse	*perdón*	car	*coche*
yes	*si*	plane	*avión*
non	*no*	airport	*aeropuerto*
what...?	*qué...?*	boat / ship	*barco*
when...?	*cuándo...?*	port / wharf	*puerto/muelle*
where...?	*dónde...?*	slow	*despacio*
there is...	*hay...*	fast	*rapido*
there is not...	*no hay...*	gas	*gasolina*
what is the time?	*Qué hora es?*	gas station	*surtidor de gasolina*
how are you?	*Cómo está?*		
		hotel	*hotel*
far	*lejos*	hostel	*albergue*
near	*cerca*	room	*habitación*
big / large	*grande*	toilets	*servicios*
small	*pequeño*	bath / shower	*baño/ducha*
new	*nuevo*	restaurant	*restaurante*
old	*antiguo/viejo*	café	*café/bar*
left	*izquierda*	table	*mesa*
right	*derecha*	chair	*silla*
first	*primero*		
last	*último*		
open	*abierto*	waiter	*camarero*
closed	*cerrado*	water	*agua*
entrance	*entrada*	bread	*pan*
exit	*salida*	drink	*bebida*
		menu	*menú*
		hot	*caliente*
bus	*autobus*	cold	*frio*

English	Spanish	English	Spanish
soup	*sopa*	north	*norte*
meat	*carne*	west	*oeste*
salad	*ensalada*	south	*sur*
bill	*cuenta*	valley	*valle*
receipt	*recibo*	mountain	*montaña*
		range	*cordillera*
		hill	*colina*
cinema	*cine*	forest	*bosque*
theatre	*teatro*	river	*rio*
pharmacy	*farmacia*	channel	*canal*
shop, store	*tienda*		
newsstand	*kiósko*		
post office	*correos*	Sunday	*Domingo*
hospital	*hospital*	Monday	*Lunes*
police	*policia*	Tuesday	*Martes*
embassy	*embajada*	Wednesday	*Miércoles*
		Thursday	*Jueves*
		Friday	*Viernes*
market, bazaar	*mercado*	Saturday	*Sábado*
how much does it cost?	*cuánto cuesta?*		
		January	*Enero*
expensive	*caro*	February	*Febrero*
cheap	*barato*	March	*Marzo*
		April	*Abril*
		May	*Mayo*
road, highway	*carretera, autopista*	June	*Junio*
street	*calle*	July	*Julio*
avenue	*avenida*	August	*Agosto*
square	*plaza*	September	*Septiembre*
alley	*callejuela*	October	*Octubre*
esplanade	*paseo*	November	*Noviembre*
bridge	*puente*	December	*Diciembre*
monument	*monumento*		
fountain	*fuente*	1	*uno/una*
church	*iglesia*	2	*dos*
palace	*palacio*	3	*tres*
fort/castle	*castillo*	4	*cuatro*
town/city	*ciudad*	5	*cinco*
village	*pueblo*	6	*seis*
museum	*museo*	7	*siete*
park	*jardin público*	8	*ocho*
		9	*nueve*
		10	*diez*
east	*este*	11	*once*

English	Spanish
12	*doce*
13	*trece*
14	*catorce*
15	*quince*
16	*dieciseis*
17	*diecisiete*
18	*dieciocho*
19	*diecinueve*
20	*veinte*
21	*veintiuno*
30	*trenta*
31	*trentiuno*
40	*cuarenta*
50	*cincuenta*
60	*sesenta*
70	*setenta*
80	*ochenta*
90	*noventa*
100	*cien*
101	*ciento uno*
110	*ciento diez*
200	*doscientos*
300	*trescientos*
400	*quatrocientos*
500	*quinientos*
600	*seiscientos*
700	*setecientos*
800	*ochocientos*
900	*nuevecientos*
1000	*mil*
2000	*dos mil*
million	*un millón*

INDEX

INDEX

*I*NDEX

NOTES

NOTES

NOTES

QUESTIONNAIRE

In our efforts to keep up with the pace and pulse of Seville, we kindly ask your cooperation in sharing with us any information which you may have as well as your comments. We would greatly appreciate your completing and returning the following questionnaire. Feel free to add additional pages. A complimentary copy of the next edition will be sent to you should any of your suggestions be included.

Our many thanks!

To: Inbal Travel Information (1983) Ltd.
18 Hayetzira Street
Ramat Gan 52521
Israel

Name: _____

Address: _____

Occupation: _____

Date of visit: _____

Purpose of trip (vacation, business, etc.): _____

Comments/Information: _____

_____

_____

_____

_____

_____

_____

_____

_____

_____

_____

_____

INBAL Travel Information Ltd.
P.O.B. 39090 Tel Aviv
ISRAEL 61390